Some Days Just Noticing

Some Days Just Noticing

by

Gary William Rasberry

WINTERGREEN STUDIOS PRESS

Wintergreen Studios Press
Township of South Frontenac,
PO Box 75, Yarker, ON, Canada K0K 3N0

Copyright © 2017 by Gary William Rasberry. All rights reserved under the International and Pan-American Copyright Conventions. No part of this book may be reproduced in any form or by electronic or mechanical means, including information storage and retrieval systems, without permission in writing from the publisher, except by a reviewer, who may quote brief passages in a review. The views expressed in this work are those of the author and do not necessarily reflect those of the publisher.

Wintergreen Studios Press (WSP) gratefully acknowledges the financial support received from Wintergreen Studios.

Every effort has been made to acknowledge the copyright holders, artists, photographers, and authors whose work appears in this text for permission to reprint material. We regret any oversights and we will be happy to rectify them in future editions.

Edited by Phil Hall and Bruce Kauffman
Book and cover design by Diane Black
Front cover art: Heidi Mack
Composed in Book Antiqua and Candara, typefaces designed by Monotype Typography and Gary Munch, respectively

Library and Archives Canada Cataloguing in Publication
Rasberry, Gary William. 1959—
Some Days Just Noticing/Gary William Rasberry

ISBN: 978-0991872268

    1. Poetry – Canadian.

    I.   Title. Some Days Just Noticing
Legal Deposit – Library and Archives Canada

I have a thirsty fish in me that can never
 find enough of what it is thirsty for.

— Rumi

July 1

It's always somebody's birthday: a nation, a neighbour, a sister, brother, father, mother. Bake a cake. Fly a flag. Put up the big top tent. Rent a marquee. Hire a band. Sing. Dance. Cut the rug. Count the candles. Count your blessings. Make sure there's a poet on hand to help mark the occasion.

July 2

July is a bright flag waving. People gather together in droves to celebrate with little or no advance notice. At the drop of June's hat, the festivities begin. Pick a festival any festival: The Roses are About to Bloom Festival, The Home Made Jam Festival, The Festival of Lesser Known Saints, The Partial Lunar Eclipse Festival, The Nearly Naked Festival, The Festival For Pet Iguana Owners. These and other less well-known festivals trumpet July.

July 3

Where will your heart take you today? How much travel until you recognize that familiar tug? Will you follow? The path is laid down while walking. Best to start now.

July 4

Where is the poem that lives in you today? Leafy shadows dance on the red brick wall across the narrow lane. There are birds out back. Always birds. Ever busy chatting and typing little notes to themselves. Is this the year the cherry tree bears fruit? The cicadas are busy adding drone to the backdrop. The monarch butterflying by—a haiku waiting to happen. Whatever form it takes, and it doesn't have to rhyme, you are being written.

July 5

"You're stuck. Really stuck. But you're through the worst of it. The next part is going to happen very quickly." This is what the psychic said before you even sat down. Before you even exchanged hellos. Cosmic therapy is not for the birds. Nor is choosing Light and Love. "Dumb it down," she said, "Dumb it down." "Start learning how to crawl again. Find a good colouring book and grab some crayons." The next part is going to happen very quickly.

July 6

The hollyhocks love it best when the heat is on. And the time is now. Light of the most exquisite variety blesses the garden. The courtyard flooded with summer. Various gardeners have been heard to say that hollyhocks make great background companions for shorter plants but we know better. The hollyhock is a teenager with a taproot. Growth spurts that might be awkward for some plants become the hollyhock. Please don't try to tell the hollyhock what to do or where to go. If it wants to be in the front row it will simply grow its way there, angling for attention. Hollyhocks, like humans, are best when their roots aren't disturbed.

July 7

She promised him a year's worth of poem but that was before she got to know him. And now it's a bit more complicated than that. Things went south. Things went flat. Promises can be hard to keep. Winners win. Losers weep.

July 8

Your baby is borrowing your car. Your baby who is no longer a baby is driving your car. This young man borrowing your car is, of course, not able to glance in the rear-view mirror and see himself in the backseat, sippy cup in hand, a toddler happy and oblivious to the dictates of traffic. But *you* are. Look. There he is in the back seat. There he is in the front seat. Here you are, adjusting the rear view mirror.

July 9

Made the mistake of listening to the news this morning. We're killing each other. Killing each other. Killing each other. In every country, every city, every town, every village. Strangers and loved ones. Loved ones and strangers. We're aiming and firing. Aiming and firing. Pulling the trigger again and again and again. This is not news but I made the mistake of listening to it this morning.

July 10

These words belong to no date in particular. These words amount to nothing more than changing the oil every requisite number of kilometers traveled. These words left this morning before breakfast. These words came ashore this afternoon. Washed up on the rocks. These words are lost luggage looking for a traveler. These words propagate and take over the page. These words run for cover. These words are why words are necessary. These words wish there was something more to add.

July 11

Sixteen sailboats on the water. The white sails are poems that take the shape of the wind. Summer sun skips across the waves and the water. Sadness gets left on the shoreline. But it seems there is always someone left behind. There you are high on a hill. Looking out across the harbour. Nothing is being asked of you and there's no reason to take blue literally but there seems to be little wind in your sails.

July 12

Make just one change each day. It can be for the better if you like.

July 13

Sheet lightning and a handful of stars. An open field full of rusted cars. Follow the river down into your heart. Carve your words into beautiful art. Naïve and trusting. Bent but not rusting. Hold fast while everything turns. Light years away a single star burns. God only knows what you're thinking of. Holding on as always for love.

July 14

Every day I stare at the world. These are the words of poet Mary Oliver: *Every day I stare at the world.* Never has the poet's job description been so concise. She nailed it. Nailed the interview. Got the job. The morning air is dense and heavy. A warm wind moves through the trees speaking in a language I must have let go of as a child. Nothing can be done for it now. A darkening sky moves the clouds about, makes snap decisions on moisture content and colour. The week has been a sky full of broken promises. I am here just noticing how low the ceiling of the world. I lie down in the grass next to Mary Oliver. *I am thinking,* she says, *maybe just looking and listening is the real work.*

July 15

Every day. This is the key, yes? Every day. Every day, you write it down. Sometimes as you see it. Sometimes as you wish it might be. Want it to be. But every day you write it down. Plant your garden, make breakfast for your children, hang the laundry, shovel the sidewalk, cut the grass, pay your bills, write your lists, do your work, offer up a prayer, give your love. If you don't write it down who will know every day?

July 16

You take me down deep. Deep into beauty. You take me down to a deeper sense of duty. Deep like the forest. Deep like the ocean. A deep that sets everything in motion.

July 17

Existentially, yours. That's how she signed every letter. It's going to get worse and it's going to get better. A lot of the casualties are a case of attrition. A lot of the talk is of the human condition. Nothing for granted, nothing for sure. Nothing a good worry stone wouldn't cure.

July 18

Mary Oliver gently reminds me that the poem will wait for me. For as long as it takes, even. If it's not over there, it's likely right here. "And Vice versa," she might add, "Vice versa." She, who possesses such an eye for beauty, suggests it might be more a matter of listening than looking. Oh, Mary. Oh, for your patience. Grace turns each and every page of yours I visit. Eight decades of living a life with only these instructions: *Pay attention. Be astonished. Tell about it.*

July 19

Everything changes when the train starts moving. The sweep of landscape out the window brings a certain stillness to the traveler. It's a temporary Zen quickly abandoned when the conductor starts taking tickets and making announcements for the next stop. Meantime let go to the beautiful blur of trees fields forests barns clouds roads. Live in the 'Nothing but Now.' Free-floating and fastened to the horizon.

July 20

But the airport. The airport is a horse of a different colour. If the train is a rocking chair, the plane is a catapult. Strap yourself in and prepare to be launched unceremoniously into the friendly skies. Poets need not apply.

July 21

On advice provided by Environment Canada's weather service: *Never leave people or pets inside a parked vehicle.* In case you weren't aware, the weather report tells us there is a Heat Warning in Effect. *Hot and humid conditions continue today. High temperatures are in the low thirties with humidex values approaching 40.* Any excuse not to write, I hear you saying. And, today, you would be right. *Frequently visit neighbours, friends and older family members, especially those who are chronically ill, to make sure they are cool and hydrated.* Or to share the shade of a poem. And perhaps it goes without saying but the mind can play tricks in the heat: Never read poetry to people or pets inside a parked vehicle.

July 22

A hardcover is not required. Nor a dust jacket with advance praise for the poet. Just the words themselves. Falling out in lines just so. In a way that might find you here. Language and love in careful measure, the last part of day slipping away until it's time to light the lamp and welcome evening.

July 23

A good thing you were there to help set the sun this evening. Help grow the shadows and silhouette the skyline. Darken the waves. Cast the last light across the water. Light the lanterns that now glow from the ferryboat and blue-black the sky behind it. Give the moon a gentle hand up and start to think about hanging a star or two before you call it a night. A lot to do in one sitting. A good thing you were there to help.

July 24

This is the part where the door opens and someone unexpected introduces herself. This is the part where you wish you'd said something sparkling and original. This is the part where the story starts to trail off and become something other than the story you were trying to tell. This is the part where you realize there is no dress rehearsal.

July 25

This is the part where you wonder whose credit card they're using to fund the project. This is the part where, after this part, certain parts will fall into place while other parts will remain out of reach and resist the parts you were hoping would come together. This is the part where you wait and wait and wait for your name to appear as the credits roll.

July 26

I have a row of books stacked atop the piano in my studio. Books filled with poems, artfully displayed and thoroughly read. Don Domanski and Robin Blaser. Bukowski's *Bone Palace Ballet*. The collected poems of Seamus Heaney and e. e. cummings. Steven Heighton. Adrienne Rich, Sharon Olds, Lorna Crozier—even Joni Mitchell is here—though she spends most of her time in the music section. My 18-year-old son spends hours at this piano. His conversations with Schumann, Brahms, Brubeck and Bach are music to my ears. My son doesn't read my books but he makes poetry with his hands while Al Purdy, Wendell Berry and Anne Michaels look on approvingly.

July 27

One or two bumblebees wrap up the last of their work before going off-line. The sky pales and evening comes on. The garden falls silent save for the crickets just beginning their shift. The dragonflies would love to call it a night but the mosquitoes are out and there is still work to be done. The sky pales and evening comes on. Sitting on the porch in a comfortable chair, your day is also coming to an end. This is why porches were built and this is what people are meant to do at this time of day. The sky pales and evening comes on.

July 28

Today is today. A certainty of sorts while it's still today. According to yesterday, it will mean very little tomorrow. Today is today.

July 29

Low tide today. Looking up friends on index cards. Pacing the cage. Staring into the mirror. Both sides now. Signing up for self help seminars. Embracing various clichés one day at a time. Eschewing all the old tapes. Making a new recording of positive beliefs and affirmations: You Are Enough.

July 30

I could go deeper but I'm not quite there yet. Not so good at landing without a net. I'm better when I'm coming down. Reel-to-reel without the sound. Imagining life other than real time. Imagining yours. Imagining mine. Now imagine ourselves as if we were there. The wind on the water. The wind in our hair. It's just by chance the two of us are dreamers. Floating just like party streamers. Romantic and stubborn. Quiet and wind torn. Some pretend and some for real. Some of the time is part of the deal.

July 31

We are all made different by the things we notice and don't notice. See and don't see. Feel and don't feel. The boy on the bike. The kids on the corner. The parked car with its open windows. Chalk on the sidewalk. August thumbing through the last pages of July.

August 1

21st century canoeing on a Saturday afternoon. Out for a solo paddle on a bright blue lake. A loon with his red eye pops up on the surface just off to my right. To my left, a motorboat pulls a teenaged water skier. In the time it takes for the wake to reach both my canoe and the loon, I'm using my cell phone as a personal flotation device. Interesting where you can and can't get coverage.

August 2

Year upon year upon year. So long now. But I'm finding my way back. I'd love to blame someone. Blame you for taking up so much room at the inn. It's not a simple matter. It's not difficult, either. It takes one to know one, I suppose. And if you want more cryptic go ahead and dare me to. I bought in without a down payment on the timeshare. You took credit for anything I wanted to be. What a difficult challenge for so sensitive a creature. I wanted the cake but lost my appetite. You are a solitude. Large as life. Amazing, really. It's hard to know what to feel. I am beginning to see you. Can you see me? I'm finding my way back. So long now.

August 3

What Frank Said: *Daylight is an ugly time of day. So many people are awake. Stupidity is replicating itself at an astonishing rate. Nobody looks good wearing brown lipstick. I really don't like to talk. It's like exercise for me. A converted shoe store in Norwalk with a beer license also fired us. This was the only R&B band in the entire Mojave Desert at that time.* Amazing how Frank turns to poetry without even trying. Doing poetry as only Zappa can do poetry.

August 4

Teach me again how to dive deeper. How to surface from time to time. And that part about the dark and the light. Remind me. How few words. How much time. These are not questions. These are not demands. Bend without breaking. Mindful and deliberate. Well worn. Never worn out. A turn of phrase and a trick of the light.

August 5

It's mostly when you're driving and you're somewhere between here and there. Somewhere between there and here. Mostly in-between. The road that curves around the blue lake without waves. Forested rock cuts rise on the left. Water lapping on the right. Language lives on this road. Lives in this in-between place where one never arrives. Words come to visit. Some decide to stay. Others you never hear from again. Thinking and not thinking. Writing poems in mid-air. Mostly when you're neither here nor there. [Post Script: If you remove the 't' from 'there' you end up here. In this way, here will always be just a consonant away from there. Surely enough room for poetry to live with/in the difference.]

August 6

How hot? How dry? A cicada could start a fire on a day like today. July was an anvil and August continues to be the hammer. Gardens limp not lush. Brown trees losing their leaves. Living things dying. That's how hot. That's how dry.

August 7

Remembering the little I know of BW: *The stubborn particulars of grace*. I imagine Bronwen walking these Kingston streets. Years and years past and not so long ago. Store front windows. Café quiet. Looking out. Looking in. Were her poems tea-steeped or did coffee fuel her visits with the Muse? Someone around here surely knows the answer. A close reading of *Signs of the Former Tenant* now long overdue.

August 8

Those who paint pictures and those who spin stories. Those who travel so far to bring us all home. Those who draw our eyes to the horizon. Those who might tell us how we got here in the first place.

August 9

Give yourself an out and you might take it. If you sing 'Twist and Shout' just don't fake it. If it's a poem you want you must make it. Such are the ways of the world. If you never travel you never see. You can't hold on and still be free. If life unravels let it be. Such are the ways of the world. You meet a stranger and show your heart. You come together you come apart. You find the ending you find the start. Such are the ways of the world.

August 10

Hold a cliché and speak to it softly. Pass through language and polish the stone. Gather the words loosely together. In love with the world and never alone.

August 11

Love. Never leave home without it.

August 12

It's time for a field trip to NYC. Off you go. A border so big one can't help but trip over it. Easily. But not without noticing difference in the sameness. The United States of America. A country like no other. Variations on a theme: Red Blue & White — Red splotches spooling across a Blue sky. Some White clouds thrown in for effect. And the film begins. Silent. If only. Traffic builds. By the dawn's early light. Pride of ownership and self-preservation. Land of the Free. Factory-installed everything. A country like every other.

August 13

Late afternoon light glints off the Hudson. Sliding south, coach class, down the valley made famous by what waits for us at the mouth. An uninterrupted train of thought. Enough green to make one forget how much glass and concrete and steel await. Place names begin to make history. The river widening. The Palisades appear on the far shore. A canyon forming to draw us in to a world that must be seen to be believed.

August 14

What did you expect from The Village at this hour? Of course the city never sleeps. Well, it sort of does. People sleep in shifts. And yet at 4am the fire escape is like a cliffside seat. Village rituals enacted. Drunken anthropologists still have an eye for detail.

August 15

Canyons. Urban steep. Glass and steel. Echo. It's very late. It's very early. Disorderly and Drunk. Industrial vehicles backing up somewhere. Always. Reverse signals and short siren blasts from police cars are omnipresent. And the heat of the day still holding the night air hostage. Neighbourhood bars. Urban saloons. Underground Velvet Speak Easy. Sanitized now but still hoping Lou might show up any minute. Another round of shots. And just enough for cab fare.

August 16

The Book of Questions leaves room for doubt:
> *What could someone figure out about you by the friends you've chosen? What are the most important things (excluding children) you've brought into the world that would not exist without you?*

Answers are questions imagining themselves otherwise.

August 17

Quick-scan your shelves for titles that jump out:
The Hidden Room. Heartbreak Therapy. Scream Blue Living. Blood, Tin, Straw. The War in Heaven. The Politics of Postmodernism. When Things Fall Apart. The Pleasure of the Text. Why be Happy When You Can be Normal? Ideology and Curriculum. Signs of the Former Tenant. Men in the Off Hours. Bone Palace Ballet. Meeting the Shadow. Dick and Jane: We Play and Pretend. The Salamander Room. The Mountain that Loved a Bird. My Many Coloured Days. Rainbow Fish to the Rescue. The Missing Piece. Lily's Purple Plastic Purse. The Quiltmaker's Gift. Hope is an Open Heart. The Starship and the Canoe.. Inventing the Hawk. The Cure for Death by Lightning.

That will be all for today.

August 18

The slow turning has begun. Yes, we're always turning. There are scientific explanations. There are formulas. The flat earth theory has been given a pink slip. Newton never fell far from the tree. At least that's what Galileo said. If Neil really was up there he certainly took some fabulous photographs. One small step and the image of a blue green ball floating. And that's my point I suppose. The earth is spinning and we feel the turning. I know I do. It's like clockwork. Check the calendar. Notice the light. Notice the shadows. Grace takes its place. We're turning. Slowly. Away and toward. And the earth reminds us it's time. It's time once again. To take stock. To listen if you've been talking too much. Speak if you've been silent. It's happening. Right now. The slow turning has begun. Once again it's time.

August 19

Please don't let them tell you how to: Think. Write. Listen. Invest. Vacation. Work. Or what to: Read. Eat. Drink. Sing. Write. Think. Because they will. Yes, they will. And it won't necessarily be menacing or even mean. But they will. Because they have to. Because there will always be a They. And you will always be a You. It will be For Your Own Good. That's what they'll say. And how you respond will dictate the kinds of poems you write…

August 20

… So just let go of the line and let it feed out behind you as you move forward without looking back. Awkward and graceful. Steady and uncertain. Purposeful. Enjoy using the word 'spool.' The line slipping through your hands, like time, without the sense of loss. Eat. Drink. Write. Listen. Work. Play. Sing. Invest. Vacation if you must. And please don't listen to a word of this. I have no idea who's talking.

August 21

Rainy days are a reminder. Love the sky for all its moods. Love the sky for giving the sun the day off. Slow down. Love the feeling that holds you closer to your source. Love the feeling that makes rest seem like the perfect plan.

August 22

Here's one for sadness. No matter what the date. For you: I know you are. For me: I know I am. We all are. Some days. No matter what the date. And today is that day.

August 23

I wish you weren't so hard on yourself. I wish you could see how it might feel to be good enough. Better than good, even. You do not have to do anything to be loved. And you are.

August 24

As long as you write it down. Then you'll know. This matters. Ambiguous antecedent and all. It's all that matters: This. Write it down. For as long as you are able. For as long as you can.

August 25

Let us give thanks and praise for caffeine. The sanctioned recreational drug of poetic champions composing. Van the Man knew of what he spoke: *Give me my rapture today.*

August 26

Always the question: Where to start? Always the reply: Here, of course. No job too big or small. Small fascinations are big around here.

August 27

A soft breeze pianos the leaves into a Sonata. Layers of late summer green lull us into believing that this might last forever. Beethoven, eyes closed: Sonata #30 in E major, Op. 109 III. *Tema e variazioni.* Yes, this might last forever.

August 28

If you had to put your finger on what makes this life so sweet? Stumbling and articulate. Counting your blessings. No need to spell-check Gratitude. Eyes closed. Smiling the day into being. Running your hands over the map. Going by feel. No matter the topography. Ouija-boarding your way across the stippled surface that spirits the message: You are Here.

August 29

Prayers for the poet who goes deeper than what language would allow. The work more like a strange tear that wrenches her from anything familiar. Leaves her isolated and alone until sometime later when it's safe, and the coast is clear and we choose to connect.

August 30

Close your eyes and imagine late afternoon sunlight that dances out across the water. Out and out to the horizon where some kind of blue is made possible by a late August alchemy of water and sky. Try not to use the words 'diamond' or 'sparkle,' 'summer' or 'dazzle.' Then proceed to break your own rules with the help of Bruce Cockburn: *All the diamonds in this world that mean anything to me are conjured up by wind and sunlight sparkling on the sea.*

August 31

Last days of summer going down slow. Melancholy need not apply despite the sun's reluctance to appear. Cool and overcast is the perfect fit. Lots of grey to mix the blues and greens together. This is not the goodbye kiss we'll remember.

September 1

One tired leaf butterflies its way to earth. A haiku-worthy moment knowing thousands and thousands of others are dying to do the same.

September 2

Any and all autumnal thoughts melt in a heat that staggers. Google tells us these are not the dog days of summer. Turns out the Greeks and Romans were pointing to Sirius, the Dog Star, who appeared in the heavens just as the earth was heating up, making July unbearable in the Mediterranean. A celestial bark as bad as its bite: it was a signal to all who paid attention to such things to prepare for catastrophe, fever and other impending disasters. Mad dogs and Englishmen take note.

September 3

The heat. The heat. And so we are not yet ready to put our clothes back on. And in this university town, the young—who flood back to assume their first week's worth of irresponsibility—are more than willing to wear less. Pacemaker advisory in effect for the unsuspecting men well beyond attending classes of any sort who may or may not recall the heat of their own youth.

September 4

Let us give thanks and praise to the poets, the songwriters, the miners and the deep-sea divers who present us with offerings of language dismantled. Language turned on its head. Language spun through a prism. Language turned inside out so that we might struggle with not-knowing. Glimpse ourselves familiar and unrecognizable. Bear witness to a world that is and is not ours to name.

September 5

Caution: Word Pairings Next 5 km. Mixed blessings. Sour grapes. Lost dogs. Found objects. Soft landings. Hard feelings. Scary stories. Half-truths. Good times. Bad endings. Wishful thinking. Safe arrivals. Speed bumps. Cross roads. Cross check. Criss-cross. Catch all. Loose change. Long shot. Left over. Short shrift. Easy money. Hard times. Good riddance. Bad blood. Best buy. Back pedal. Bush whack. Hard core. Soft sell. Super charged. Under sold. Over done. Well-wisher. Weight watcher. Waste deep. Wet paint. Dry spell. Sing song. Talk therapy.

September 6

Let us give praise and thanks to the reptilian brain. For heartbeat and breath. For fight or flight. For looking after autonomic affairs on our behalf. For being old and ancient beyond reason and belief. For survival. For hoarding, dominance, preening and mating. Let us give praise and thanks to the reptilian brain. For confusion. For pain and suffering. For love, fear, hate and lust. For making us irrational. For lacking language. For the reminder: we are animals and rage is part of the package. For the reminder: we are so much more than our thinking. So much more than talking heads. So much is beyond our control. And, finally, for keeping us in therapy well beyond what our rational minds would ever have wanted or believed.

September 7

Careless thoughts and pencil thin nights. Kerosene lamps light the way with wispy smudges of black to remember the dark by. There's always a hallway involved in these dreams. Choices to be made in corridors. Following the signs that aren't there. Always the presence of others along the spiritual commute. A shared rush hour in hushed tones. Some get off at Jung Street. Others choose the middle way. Such a wash of beautiful light at the edges of the dream.

September 8

Spend freely in wise ways. Wish well for others. Offer a hand up. Take up the cause of laughter. Don't be scared to cry. Breathe on a regular basis. Speak with less talking. Smile when embarrassed without apologizing. Take time to polish something silver with care. Take up a small task with full attention. Collect ideas that make things better. Give less advice. Don't wait until tomorrow.

September 9

The leaves seem to think nothing of their greenness. I can see them now from my window waving and bending every which way. Today's dance studio breeze has no intention of telling them about The Wind. How everything changes. How one day the birds stop chatting among themselves. There's something new in the air that no one mentions. There's polite laughter between squirrels when one says that orange will soon be the new green upon which one excuses itself to rush off and gather something. It's just nuts. Forage. Foliage. Forage. Forage. Forage. The breeze begins again with something to sway by. The leaves seem to think nothing of their greenness.

September 10

Conversations. Nothing but weather. Conversations. Farmer-almanacing our way around the water cooler. On street corners. Coffee shops. Backyards, too. Long cold winter coming. Again. Followed by the wringing of hands. Knowing nods. A whiff of despair. Conversations. Anything but weather. Conversations.

September 11

Some place across the ocean, refugees pour out of homes they never had. Broken and brutalized, they stumble in bloodied herds toward nothing they know. They are images on our screen. They are sound bytes in our social media'd existence. The horrors of history rip the future up into bloody pieces. In the news, we hear the refrain, "Put them on a train. Keep them moving." They are so far from home. They are like nothing we know. Meantime, over here on this day, we look up momentarily from our coffees to remember The Day the horror hit so close to home. Inconceivable to begin with—that something so heavy could fly. Made from metal with wings attached. Inconceivable in the end that so much metal could come crashing. Through fire and ash, they stumble in herds toward nothing they know. Refugees in suits and ties and the history of horror rewritten. They are so close to home. They are like nothing we know.

September 12

Finally a day of heavy rains. The spell has been broken. Winds, warm and blustery, toss summer about. Little waves on street puddles. The language of umbrellas spoken along the sidewalks. Loosely translated: there's not a lot to worry about right now but wait. Just wait. The spell has been broken.

September 13

Rain curtains the windows. A candle lights the way. Our bodies are music made for nighttime listening. The moon will not show this evening. Nor will we be watching for it. The stars have been folded into clouds for safekeeping. The windows are curtains of rain. The way lit by a candle. Music made for nighttime listening.

September 14

The light's not here to greet you in quite the same way this morning. It's not the window blinds. It's not you. It's the light. And don't expect tomorrow will be better. It's a trick of the light. The planet's tilt. A cosmic joke of sorts. Played out each year. Year in. Year out. It's a joke you'll never get used to. One you'll find less and less humorous as the years slide by. There's always plenty of light until it's dark. You're on the planetary treadmill. Not certain whether to walk faster or slower. Sunrise. Sunset. The squeeze happens at day's end, too. It's all very manageable right now. And this year might not be so bad? But it's just a matter of time. Eventually, the sun will no longer slide toward the horizon before taking a graceful bow and setting. No. Soon it will just stone drop without ceremony. And you'll stop waiting for the show. You'll wonder why you feel tired in the morning. Not quite ready to start the day. You'll wonder why you feel tired in the evening. Quite ready to end the day. Soon you'll be left in the dark. It's not you. It's the light.

September 15

You're father told you never to touch his vinyl collection. All that music encrypted and pressed into tracks where only the needle can find the groove. A library like no other. Catalogued and pristine. Even the liner notes. The weight of all that music weighing heavy on your mind. It could have been Rachmaninoff. Or maybe Miles Davis. It wouldn't matter. He'd know if you'd even slid the album from its sleeve. You would forever wonder why music would require a gatekeeper. But the height of the walls only made them that much more tempting to climb. Just a taste of the forbidden. And now — all these years later — they're all yours. The tables have been turned. Meantime your kids don't have to climb anything to listen to the sound of music. The turntable, like the typewriter, is a novelty item. Another old relic to rib dear old Dad about as they download mp3s. Of course, they can't see the music they listen to. Have no concept of the concept album. Can't imagine what went into putting certain songs on Side A. Others on Side B. Even the liner notes.

September 16

Ever have that moment when you just know? You are here for love. In this moment there is a reckoning. A dawning, not gradual. Love is why you are here.

September 17

All about love and prepositions. Love needs prepositions. Prepositions need love: About love. Around love. In addition to love. In and out of love. Outside, over and on top of love. Past love. Round love. Since love. Despite love. Through love. Throughout love. In case of love. In spite of a love. Instead of love. In place of love. Except love. Against love. After love. Across love. During love. Beneath love. Beyond love. Between love. By love. Before love. Because of love. As for love. Apart from love. Underneath love. Unlike love. Until love. Toward love. Regarding love. Within and without love. On and off love. Next love. Near love. Into love. Like love. Love love. There's nothing like. Love.

September 18

Death and dying and all the books ever written about. Death and dying. You are. I am. We are. Dying. Remember when you said, "I'm not afraid of death, it's the dying part that scares me." Interesting how The Tibetan Book of Living and Dying could become a best seller. And remember back when comedy got hold of Kubler-Ross. Co-opted and parodied her 'stages?' Good grief. How many were there? Five. Maybe it was only funny because so many never get beyond denial and anger? There's certainly nothing funny about depression. And acceptance is something even comics would die for.

September 19

Not that I'm scare of dying or anything. My body is a temple of sorts. With unbridled generosity it has taken care of me. Never thought of myself as a pilgrim. Just enjoyed walking. Even uphill sometimes. Never worried about the forest for the trees. Saw mountains for the first time. Rivers and lakes. The ocean and the desert on the same day. Just walking and walking. Blindly much of the time. And now I seem to have stumbled upon a horizon that provides just a glimpse. Death is going to be a part of my life. Not soon. He prayed. Not soon. But still. Thy Will. Not my will.

September 20

All you want is a loan you don't have to pay back. Maybe a grant awarded without the paperwork. Some money to ease your worried mind. Soften your debt. Gain some credibility. Afford an opportunity. Or even better, a patron to appear. A philanthropist who so believes in you and what you're doing. Understands that even brilliant ideas need an infusion of cash to become manifest in a world of cash-strapped ideas. All you're looking for is a break. A boost. A leg-up. You know your problems are meaningless. Trivial. Trite. You have all you want. All you need. You *are* wealthy now. You're privileged. Blessed. You want for nothing. You want it all.

September 21

No words fell from the sky today. They were up there somewhere talking quietly among themselves but must have been too busy to touch down. Maybe tomorrow.

September 22

Best just to focus on breathing today: the simplest thing that sometimes feels so difficult. Check in tomorrow for update. (See September 21 for further details.)

September 23

Speed Bump. Check the air in your tires. Maybe you're under-inflated. Or over-inflated. Over or under. It's all about the ride. Cruise control has it's pros and cons. Highway Zen offers insight into speed and its limits. Ride the ribbon slicing its way through rock cuts. Take the nearest exit. There will be a stream. A bridge. Under or over.

September 24

When does poetry break into song? Cadence leads us all down the garden path, often with enough time to smell the flowers. But rhyme, rhyme tends to beat around the bush. It breaks out when it wants to. Insists we take the tour on its terms. Lyrically speaking, when does poetry break into song?

September 25

Might 'Glorious' be reinstated into the lexicon to talk about late September days and nights? Enough sun seemingly to carry us through and hold us over until at least mid-November. Of course, we're not thinking straight but this is what the first days of Autumn are for. This warmth and brilliance of light are not, as we once suspected, a form of cruel trickery. Of course rain will decide to become sleet. The romance of frost eventually buried in brown slush. Winter-harsh is an agreed upon if not accepted convention. But maybe, just maybe, memory offers a solar-powered alternative to power us forward into what we all know is coming. Wouldn't that be Glorious?

September 26

Every song ever written about walking down a country road. *Walk on down. Walk on down. Walk on down. Walk on down a country road.* James Taylor—JT—and the forest filtering the afternoon light. The road a generous invitation into your every memory of oak and maple, pine and birch, cedar and spruce, poplar and beech. Childhood canopied in green. Light, light and more light. Friends and lovers. Lovers and friends. Down through the woods blue catches your eye. A piece of sky. A forgotten lake. The forest floor. A falling down cabin just over the ridge. Narrowing now. Tractor width. The road not even a road. *I guess my feet know where they want me to go. Walking down a country road.*

September 27

And the stars. The stars. The heavens. Here on earth you're walking across a midnight field below an ocean of stars that sweeps you off your feet and beyond any possible celestial shore. Humbled and tiny. Staggering under the weight. Pondering questions so small they disappear.

September 28

Late night thoughts can't stand the light of day. A blessing to be sure. Recall the inverse relationship between the still of night and the mind's noise. Barbed thoughts that catch and tear. An unproductive, fretful busyness. An inner clamour and an outer quiet that magnifies the sounds of your inner workings. And then dream after dream. Disquieting. Nothing restful about this kind of sleep. Then the first waking moments. Neither here nor there. Grappling. Grasping. For a clue. A pointless necessary exercise. Recall your own moments of trying to describe a dream. Everything falls apart. Words don't work when it comes to the blur of images that coat the backs of your eyes. The dream journal maybe. For those willing to mine the depths. Disrupt sleep patterns in an attempt to make night day. Tripping over and under and into the unconscious. And why is someone always chasing you?

September 29

Coffee. Coffee. Coffee. Each of us has our own way. Our own style. Sensibility. Story. Where the beans come from. How they were grown. How they were harvested. Who they were harvested by. Who bought them? Sold them? Who roasted them? For how long? And how shall the bean be prepared and administered? Crushed. Cracked. Ground. Steeped. Stewed. Expressed. Percolated. Dripped. Plunged. Pressed. Injected. Smoked. Etc. And what shall be added to the brew? Cream. Sugar. Honey. Hot water. Cold milk. Hot milk. Steamed milk. Milk foam. Or nothing. Just black. Coffee. Coffee. Coffee. There are so many ways. Class dismissed.

September 30

Remember when the word 'text 'had a scholarly ring to it? Textual underpinnings. A sea of textuality. A close reading of the text. Etc. Etc. And now? We're all walking down the street texting one another. No one appears to be looking where they're going. *Hey – did you get my text?*

October 1

Each day now, without fail, night drops in earlier and earlier. That is to say each day brings less and less of itself and more and more of night. This awareness, along with the weight the growing darkness brings, is somehow made more bearable by the neighbours along my street who have hung sparkle lights on their front porches. The darkened street is shiny-wet and autumnal. The black pavement shivery with coloured lights. More and more of us are pulling our collars up. Heads down. Seeing less and less. But the blinking fairy lights guide us home through the dark. Earlier and earlier. Later and later. Without fail.

October 2

Breath and bones and here on loan. This is the human condition. We strive to flesh out the story. Add colour and nuance. Drama and detail. This life of ours has to mean something. This must matter. Together and alone. Alone and together. *No dress rehearsal* as Gord has told us in no uncertain terms. *This is our life.* Tragically hip or otherwise. Mark each day on the calendar. Keep track in all the ways you can.

October 3

Why? What for? Why now? How come? Who knows? State these four questions followed by the single pithy response five times quickly. Repeat as needed.

October 4

If you've ever seen a hawk fly at high speed (and low altitude) across a gravel road straight into the trees then you know the urgency of flight. The nature of the beast. High lazy circles on the upper thermals are, in this case, strictly for the birds. Wingspan can be highly over-rated. In the instant I saw the hawk's trajectory, I felt for whatever was being chased down. Hunted. Whatever it was, it didn't have a prayer. Didn't stand a chance. Death came quickly somewhere in the tangle of trees. I didn't think a hawk could travel quite like that. Anyway, I'm thinking whatever it was that was being hunted down likely didn't feel a thing.

October 5

No one will know if this wasn't written on October 5. Will they? How important is it to get the date right? What is about *these* words on *this* day? How likely is it that you rode your bike through the park today while people walked their dogs when yesterday, out in the wilds, you witnessed a bird of prey intent on fulfilling its job description? The leaves here in the park haven't given a single thought to turning. Dogs are barking up the wrong trees. A quick informal survey shows that sweaters and light jackets are becoming all the rage. No poetry here. Next thing you know it will be October 6.

October 6

There must be something to write about other than coffee. I'm certain of it. A support group for people who write only about coffee, perhaps. It's not like I need coffee to write. Not at all. Certainly there is the ritual of grinding the words and tamping them down with conviction so that meaning, deep and rich, can be properly expressed. It's not as though I dive down into the poet's brew and luxuriate. Treading there, lucid and dreaming, in lines that break off into patterns all their own. There's so much world to be written. It's not like I need coffee to start the trip.

October 7

Pressure. Pressure. Pressure. Why? How? Who? When? What? Where? Why? Why? Why? All these beautiful caring people I know pushing so hard in their lives. Pushing hard on the boundaries of what is everyday doable. What *is* doable every day? Job descriptions and family matters in constant collision. Love and duty. Stress and strain. Bound by duty. Bound by love. Buoyed by love. Every day. What matters most? Work deadlines and bill payments. Feeding and clothing our children. Providing for them. Being fully there for them. Loving them as they need to be loved. Can we do it all? Every day? Can we do it all?

October 8

Mid-morning light blesses everything it touches. Store fronts, cyclists, city dwellers. Sidewalk conversations at King & Queen. Slide down a block to Market Square where kale carrots cabbage maple syrup honey fresh cut flowers and other market stall offerings await. There is a flow that is in play here. Some of us sense it. Doesn't really matter who does or doesn't. It's an autumnal Zen that reminds us of the beauty of our smallness. The planet's spin at just *this* moment. It's that 'You Are Here' moment: Big Universe. Tiny 'You' and the arrow pointing. Mid-morning light blessing everything it touches.

October 9

It's a rain and pull-your-collar-up damp kind of day. Lots of greys on the palette to choose from and an overcast canvas to paint the day upon. To add colour, city work crews are digging up the neighbour's front lawn. Again. They're using the Big Equipment. That house on the corner is just plain bad luck. A few months ago they ripped up the back yard. A few months before that it was the side yard. Sewage seeks its own level and it seems to be doing its level best to seek our neighbour's basement. It's ugly. Always the heavy machinery and open heart surgery and raw excavation. Always the diesel hum of over-sized equipment. Always the prolonged torture of tarmac and concrete being interrogated ...

October 10

… With the skin sliced open and the earth's innards exposed, we're seeing stuff we never wanted to see. We feel for these particular neighbours (maybe not as much as we are relieved not to *be* these neighbours living in their cursed home that is no different than our homes save for the sewage in the basement). There but for the Grace of The Sewage Gods go we. Our pipes work. Buried conduits that do their job invisibly and efficiently. Everybody's flushing without a thought to where it all goes. I'm beginning to think it's all going into our neighbour's basement. I don't know what this means re Karma and all but nobody gives a shit as long as it's not their basement. I'd write more but the incessant whine of the machinery and the thought of all that shit going wherever it wants have curbed my appetite for poetry. That house on the corner is just plain bad luck.

October 11

Love your neighbour as yourself. How hard can it be? Guess it depends on where you live and who your neighbour is. Guess it depends on whether your neighbour thinks the same way you do. Guess it depends on how high (or low) you build your fence. Guess it depends on how you love yourself. Guess it depends on how you love. How hard can it be?

October 12

Blue jays return to prattle and brag. Early October has hit a small snag. Summer returns in a game of tag. Forest birds flit but rarely settle. The sleeping woodstove reminds the kettle. Freight train on the outskirts — metal on metal. The days are warm but won't always be. The heat of the sun a rustle of trees. And all of the changes we still can't see. A beautiful confusion of the seasons. Red orange yellow can be so pleasing. The poet's campaign to rhyme and reason. That's why the jay is given voice. That's why we have and have no choice. The season turns — let us all rejoice.

October 13

Whatever stuff I wrote yesterday about autumn feeling like summer: forget it. Wind and rain. Rain and wind. Taking us all for a ride today. Wouldn't have it any other way. A little confusing perhaps but this is what we signed up for. Wonder what season it will be tomorrow?

October 14

Winning is so much fun. Winning makes people happy. Everyone loves a winner. Winning creates a euphoric amnesia that eradicates any and all past experiences of losing. Losing is no fun. Losing sucks. Losing makes people feel like losers when what they really want to feel like are winners. Note that it's easiest and most convenient to bear witness to others winning and/or losing on our behalf. To illustrate: follow a professional sports team that has been winning with reckless abandon for some specified period. Example 1: Try a short, jump-on-the-bandwagon trip once your franchise-of-choice is deep into a play-off run and much of the long-term pain and suffering has already been neatly avoided. Put slightly differently: wait for a winner and then love being part of the winning ride. Example 2: Try on adulation of a beloved losing franchise with whom you have suffered greatly for a very (very) long time. Witness how a profound and blinding ecstasy can take hold when losing morphs into winning. Finally, know that winning is fleeting and transitory and losing can commence without warning.

October 15

In case yesterday's entry on winning and losing was too cryptic, October is the bandwagon month for baseball. In Canada, it is entirely possible to live happily for months and months and months without giving baseball a second thought. And then, October arrives. It's possible you don't even particularly like baseball. But maybe there's an urban center not so far from you that is home to a Major League Baseball franchise that has been winning like nobody's business. And maybe they have captured the imagination of an entire nation that needs something other than an election to make them feel good. And maybe you were at a local bar last evening witnessing said baseball team win a ridiculously exciting playoff game that would launch the crowd into the next stratosphere of sheer adulation for a bunch of winners. Watching strangers hug, kiss and high five one another and witnessing the reckless happiness that indeed swept through you got you thinking: winning is so much fun.

October 16

Good day to curl up with a book. There is *no* UV index today. Nor is it likely the sun's intensity will be measured by anything but a hat and coat for the days and weeks and months to come. The wind is up and I swear I heard someone mention 'November' under her breath. A few flakes from the sky. Metallic grey is the colour of the Great Lake today. A hard and unyielding surface all the way out to Wolfe Island. Best to light the stove and take stock of the slowing down happening all around you. No killing frost yet but only the most stubborn and hardy of the harvest remains in the ground. Everyone knows what's coming but the autumn orange of it all is enough to keep us in the moment, raking leaves and finding the nearest Fall Fair. Parents bundle kids up for corn mazes and pumpkin patches. Apples for cider and pies. A good day to curl up with a book.

October 17

Trees look more and more naked. Grey wants to get inside of you. Wind pushes the clouds along. 'Brisk' becomes a handy euphemism that will wear out quickly. More grey. Colour exists somewhere out there beyond your backyard. Life is not a picture book. Napping is no longer an optional activity.

October 18

Lying in the backyard last night staring up at the maple that towers above your yard. Stripped down to its essence, the big branches without their leaves still filter the stars. Pretty much stark naked. That's how it is for the maple. And for you.

October 19

There are people milling about outside the café. Someone cuts a ribbon. Someone takes a photograph. Just enough of a crowd. Thin sunlight streams through the scene. Vivaldi paints the backdrop. October is Septembering just for today though the honeyed sun has long been watered down. Someone smiles. A big, open, give-away smile with no strings attached. It makes all the difference. The ceremony ends as quietly as it began.

October 20

Sunlight makes shadows possible. Stay in the moment. Wear an extra sweater. Maybe a scarf to match the leaves in the courtyard. The stonework on these buildings cuts lines through history. The clock strikes at city hall. Cobble-stoned streets remember the sounds of horse and carriage. Here she comes across the square to greet you. Smiling, open-armed. It's been so long. Love as it was then. Love as it is now. Starting today.

October 21

People are out there dying to connect. For meaning. For love. For eye contact, even. A tattoo doesn't necessarily qualify as wearing your heart on your sleeve though you had to bleed for it. True colours or skin deep? On a day like today it's hard to tell but easy to have some of it rub off. And what about love at first sight? Stranger things have happened.

October 22

The day is full of pictures inside and outside your head. Must be all these children you're spending so much time with. They're so full of crazy hope these children. They can see it all without standing back from the canvas. Not even the brightest colours make them flinch. There is only the flow of here and now. Step inside. Move with it. Don't try to make sense of it. The moment you start to think, Everything Stops. The day will still be full of pictures. With or without you.

October 23

Every kid was a poem or a song. And the words and notes rushed together in a big field of colour. I recall laughter. Some kids were balloons that soared higher and higher. There were blue and green and purple ones. Others were little molecules happy just to collide and connect. No one seemed quite certain of what was to happen next. *Ashes. Ashes. We all fall down.*

October 24

Astonished by kids. In love with the fierceness of their intelligence. Their endless capacity to love. Tiny pebbles on the beach. Light on the surface of the water.

October 25

Age is a numbers game. It matters. It doesn't matter. The mathematics of aging. Constant addition with never a mention of subtraction. Unless you count loss. You're as old as you feel. Sign up here for this time-limited offer of free clichés: *Time is a rubber band. All in due time. Time after time. Time and time again. There's no time like the present.* Time. It matters. It doesn't matter. Hurry now, this offer could end without notice. Some restrictions may apply. Somewhere, some noteworthy person once said, *How old would you be if you didn't know how old you were?*

October 26

Rain in the gutters. Leaves fall hard outside the window. There's no dance. No whimsy. No colourful fluttering for these leaves. Just a straight drop. A fall from the sky. Like they've been shot. The poets have all gone inside to warm themselves by the fire. Check back tomorrow for further developments.

October 27

Rain warning in effect. The rain can fall harder and today it does. Hard to imagine there are arid parts of the world that receive as little as 1-3 mm of rain in a year. In case you're wondering, the Atacama Desert is one such place. In fact, there are some areas of the Atacama that have not received rainfall for periods of up to 4 years. These kinds of fun facts can quickly open into a colloquium on aridity but right now it's raining cats and dogs. In fact it's possible that 1-3 mm of rain accumulated in the time it took these words to fall on the page. *Rain rain go away. Come again another day.* By the way, the Atacama Desert is located just south of the Peru-Chile border for those who find rain hard to swallow.

October 28

Wind warning in effect. It's not enough to rip the leaves from the trees. Better to blow them into the next county over. Sun pops out for a few moments, making believe it's September. Dark clouds take over an instant later. Time lapse in real time. Overcoats parachute and pull their owners crazily down the street. Was that a cat that just blew by? What would Dorothy do besides break into song? It all spells November. People begin to make serious wardrobe adjustments. Sensible jackets are suddenly in demand.

October 29

I never meant for this to become a weather journal. I really didn't. Something about dating the entries seems to have somehow pulled the words into lines of clouds. Sun and wind and words. The poetry of weather. On any given day it simply comes down to noticing. Wind on water. A stand of tamarack. What's the sky doing? When will the moon show? Anyone seen the sun? Composing each day without the benefit of standard notation. Fretting the days like tablature. The pitch denoted implicitly. Where do we place our fingers to generate the notes? Hard to sense the music based on the score alone. But that's the weather of poetry for you.

October 30

Here we are in traffic. How many lanes? Who are all these people? What are we doing? Where are we going? How important is it to get there on time? How important are we? How long 'till this traffic light changes? Don't even bother making eye contact. Ever notice how no one drives a 'beater' anymore? Everything is brand new. Kids today don't even know what a rust bucket is. Roadwork and construction never ends. Yielding is for losers. Everyone seems to be turning left up ahead. This is how we're spending our lives.

October 31

A day to spend in the graveyard. Walking slow. Taking proper time to think and feel and notice earthly detail. Life and death and the wind bending the bare branches of the trees along the ridge. From up here you can see the river. Running slow now. Otherwise, it's dead quiet.

A Friend Forever. So Small so Sweet so Young.
Beloved. Missed. Love is Eternal.
In Loving Memory. Forever with the Lord.

Taking time for gravestone mathematics. Looking for the oldest. The youngest. The numbers carved deep enough in stone to outlast death.

A tiny flower lent not given, to bud on Earth and bloom in Heaven.
Born August 5, 1903 — Died July 14, 1905

Peace is thine and sweet remembrance is ours.
Born October 1, 1893 — Died June 7, 1984

Trying to imagine, as I tour from stone to stone, what brought birth and death together to form one story. The stories behind the numbers. Story after story. A cluster of white pine on the hill. Sky and earth. Taking proper time.

November 1

Sunrise: 6:45 AM   Sunset: 4:54 PM

Daylight savings and other oxymorons. Light—its gradual death and eventual disappearance has been well covered by poets, astrologers, spiritualists and scientists. The Mystery of Light has certainly not escaped this poet's I. Along with coffee and weather, light finds itself reflecting, shining, feathering, filtering, shadowing and generally lighting up entry after entry in this collection of days. (See September 14 and October 1 for serious foreshadowing of the euphemistically named daylight savings.) And we all knew this was coming, this night of nights when we would *Fall Back*. And we all know that daylight is worth saving. Perhaps what we don't know is what is being asked of us as the planet turns us away from the light. What does the dark have to show us about light? How shall we live knowing that the dark is light that's turning?

November 2

Another evening spent wearing songs on my sleeve. Six strings and just enough bodies to make it worth the giving. Playing it by ear. As ever. There's always someone out there waiting patiently to remind me why I do this.

November 3

I suppose global warming counts as a weather entry? And, yes, I'm drinking coffee as I write. So there's nothing new under the sun save for the fact that today the sun seems to be making things warmer when things are supposed to be getting cooler. Frost-bitten Canadians love to joke about the possible fringe benefits of global warming forgetting that, in addition to cataclysmic and disastrous environmental consequences, our weather will be primarily characterized by instability and unpredictable storms. Meanwhile, it certainly is lovely and warm out today.

November 4

He's gone now. From the public eye at least. A deposed dictator in a democracy who never looked good in sheep's clothing. Gone. Dethroned. Unseated. Toppled. Done like dinner. Only now, that we're trying on smiles once again, breathing easier, acting just a bit kinder, does it become clear how bad things had become. How mean-spirited. The New Guy will be an easy target. The old regime was a paint-by-number ruling party. The Old Guy saw us all as targets lacking only for the bull's eyes his government would paint us with. He didn't have anyone killed, just labeled and filed for tax purposes. The New Guy will eventually lose his lustre. He will become less and less new. He will be worn down. But today is today and you don't have to be cruel to be kind. We're trying on smiles. We're not missing The Old Guy. He's gone now.

November 5

When things fall apart it means that they are no longer holding together. No one has to tell you this can be an extremely uncomfortable place to be. And things do fall apart. At different times, in different ways, to varying degrees. Your body, your career, your family, your relationships, your life. And what will you do? Pema Chodron, who speaks to me from the pages of her Buddhist musings, tells me falling apart is a kind of testing and also a kind of healing. Yes, things fall apart. Then things come together. Then things fall apart again. *Can we leave enough room for not knowing how it's all going to work out?*

November 6

No more fresh cut flowers at your favourite market stall. The soil being turned over now. Frost has taken care of the leftovers. Be on the lookout for warmer socks. Reacquaint yourself with root vegetables. Stock up on tissues. Bring up the board games from the basement. Prepare to hunker down. Happily. We all know where this is heading.

November 7

Anyone who knows me — knows I'm not a quitter. And seeing me in these socks — knows I'm not a knitter. Anyone who knows me — knows me just a little. Sometimes quite tender — sometimes quite brittle. Some who know me — know what I'm not. Some have questioned a little — some quite a lot. No one knows me like I don't know me. At least with any certainty. Sometimes original — sometimes store bought. Still just learning to give what I've got.

November 8

Fear and its loyal companions spend the day in my head. Many competing voices badger and poke with a sharp stick. I've heard it all before but I listen anyway. Who is speaking and how did they get this number? On my knees now, they don't have a prayer. Couldn't hold a candle to your love.

November 9

Don't let the day get away. Move down through the pines as the late season sun goldens the path. Lights up the fallen needles that blanket the ground. Lose track of it all. Whose life? What forest? Why now? Who in the world? Wood smoke and memory. Move down through the pines until the day begins to slip just below the horizon. They're calling for frost tonight.

November 10

Box stores do not help us think outside the box. Box stores box us in. Put us in boxes. Chain us to the Pursuit of Prosperity. Compel us to pursue the dream of happiness through consumption where the world is our wastebasket. There is a quiet hell both in and outside the box store. Box stores masquerading as friendly havens are really mean islands set in oceans of parking lots. It's come down to this: Black Friday every day of the year. One evening sometime soon, try making the following mistake on purpose: pretend you don't own a car and set out on foot, preferably at night into the Land of Box Stores. You will feel lost. Take caution. Cars will not be aware of you as they shark their way back and forth. You don't exist. These places are made for vehicles only. Keep walking. The distances will be immense. As you go, you might find a dark place inside you that will never be lit by the storefront facades nor all the glowing objects within. If you get close enough, try not to catch your reflection in the automatic doors made possible by the garish light. You might mistake yourself for someone else. Someone miserable or happy.

November 11

I don't know who is remembering what on this day. Local schools dutifully hold Remembrance Day assemblies. "Lest We Forget" prominently displayed in foyers across the country. I heard one kid say, "Forget what?" Yes. What to forget and what to remember? My father fought in WWII. I fought to understand what he might have gone through. He never said a word and I never quite knew how or what to ask him. The generation gap swallowed us whole. My father is long departed, the silence still unbroken. I am remembering him today having forgotten what I really wanted to ask him. Kids everywhere assemble for moments of silence.

November 12

Isn't all medicine alternative? Looking for an alternative to illness? Where is the frame? How far do we stand back to question what we're seeing? Climb the mountain of pills and scree-slide down the other side feeling dizziness and an odd certainty. You tell the pharmaceutical reps you've decided to go to the jungle for healing with a note from your doctor. The path is slick and slippery. Fires burn all night long. Smoke sifts through the trees and slips up and up through the canopy. Will it be covered by health care?

November 13

No piece of sky left unclouded today. Grey pushes down on everything. Inside and outside my head. The barometric pressure is making unilateral decisions. A tattered flag over there tells some kind of story to the pale wind. It's a day where clouds scud. All the buildings are tacky facades. Cardboard cutouts. Rain never quite starts and never quite stops. It's a day to use two hands to hold your mug of tea.

November 14

Some days just noting the date and writing it down counts in the same way getting out of bed each morning is an act of courage and hope. With no real idea of where it's all going or how it will unfold. Some scratch marks in the dirt. A mark on the wall to document the hour, the day, the moment. Some days just noticing.

November 15

What about a different approach? Write to expose the shallowness of your thoughts. How little you know about anything. How uncool you can really be. How hard you try to keep everything in place so no one will notice any of your shortcomings. A poetry of vulnerability and insecurity and rawness. Begin writing now.

November 16

Just re-read November 15. Realized there's nothing at all different about that approach. Indeed, it's what I do every time I write. Perhaps this is where Grace comes in. Puts in a good word with the Muse after bearing witness to my consistent application of stubbornness and determination where the mundane is concerned. A certain willingness on my part to work the wheel noted by those who keep track of such things. From time to time, then, the words lift off the page in some approximation of astonishment. A poetry of vulnerability and insecurity and rawness and another reason to begin writing now.

November 17

When November cracked in half I saw you staring down the dark road. No moon to speak of. Stars somewhere but not here. Black spruce silhouettes. Marsh and bog freezing up on either side. A black bear would lope not lumber on this kind of night. You must be telling yourself to remember everything. A pair of barred owls move further into the bush. Sound hollows out your night vision. A freight train so far gone. That dream where the moose crashes through the tangle. Never so haunted and lonely as when you speak of what is to come. The longest night when your shadow comes round to meet you.

November 18

Somewhere but not here. The owls. The black bear. The dark road. The stars. The train. The black spruce. The dream. Memory and remembering. Further and further you must be telling yourself. So far gone. Only the silence you've always heard when you speak of what is to come.

November 19

Some days it's a piece of chalk. Some days a chainsaw. Always looking for work. Work that plays itself out in purposeful ways that bend and curve. A map without instructions. Each new day searching and seeking out a good place, the right time, the perfect toy or tool. Calligraphy. Cut and paste. Word count. Wood cut. Watercolour. Tool and die. Pen and ink. Pointillism. Paint by number. Etch-a-Sketch. My kingdom for a magic marker.

November 20

High winds stir the night sky. A confusion of stars. Stumble outside and grab the first star you can find. Throw it like a rock through a window. You know you're going to hit something. Break something wide open you didn't know was closed to you. A kind of cosmic smash and grab. This sort of celestial vandalism isn't new. And November's jealous lover always steals a constellation and always gives it back again. See it hang there now over the field, a bit bent out of shape. We're all spinning fast. If you fall down get right back up again.

November 21

Close your eyes but don't shut the world out. Swing the heavy gate of your heart open. Make a candle of yourself and pray for the world. For everyone and everything in it. It's much too big a task but the tiny flame that holds the light suggests otherwise.

November 22

What if your five-year-old became special advisor to the Prime Minister's office? What if your border collie offered pithy bits of wisdom and poetry each day during your morning walk? What if your cat openly apologized for all those times it acted smug and superior? What if your city was given over to green space? What if daycare workers were paid more than lawyers? What if the new suicide bombers strapped belts of coloured balloons and soap bubbles to themselves and detonated them in public squares as celebratory peace offerings? What if 'yes' became the new 'no'? What if getting ahead meant walking beside? What if we gave peace a chance? What if we started right now?

November 23

The poet's song does not always sing the world into a place of unison or harmony. The notes are often hard to hear. Difficult. Dissonant. Beyond our capacity to sing them ourselves with any degree of comfort. But never discount the possibility of a single note changing everything. It's the same light that pours through the shattered stain glass window.

November 24

Poet writes rhyming couplets on a plane headed for South America: We all walk out to the end of the wing. To listen to the pilot sing. A song we thought we knew so well. But with the wind in our ears it's hard to tell. A blue wash of moon. The ocean's swell. In the black of night it's hard to tell.

November 25

Add this to your poem: the sound of water making its way down the mountain. Ceaseless and noisy like your thoughts. And birdsong. Don't forget the birdsong. Sweetening the morning. The Peruvian light of a quality that asks for nothing yet demands something more. Words don't do the trick. The pen hovers—wondering how it might be possible to bring The Here here. Capture The Now for later.

November 26

As is so often the case, I don't know where I am. A lush garden in a deep valley. Dizzy just to crane my neck to take in the tops of the mountains. The impossible shear face that drops down to where I sit. I am in a place I've never been feeling as though I am in other places I've never been: Nepal. Vietnam. Nicaragua. China. I don't know why this is so. But I will add this to my poem.

November 27

Evening light that dazzles. Leaves that vibrate and sway. The dance of shadows. The dizziness. Something ancient. Tiny birds that would fit in your pocket, sing to you in Spanish. Translators of your dreams. Little songs and sounds that begin to turn day into night. The Peruvian family climbs the steep road back up from the fields. Children carrying large bundles of cilantro. The light falling hard.

November 28

The yellow dog of Peru starts up like a lawnmower and the day begins. A source of consternation for those who may have come here to be contemplative. It turns out that the yellow dog of Peru, who lives here in the deep bowl of this valley, starts up like a lawnmower through the night hours as well — indiscriminately it would seem. His 'starting up' is enough for his two companions to join him in this particular form of canine discourse. So now we possess 3 dog-power capability here in the Sacred Valley. For what I do not know. This is the part of the story the dogs, despite their incessant barking, cannot write. Yet there is some sense that the yellow dog knows more than he is willing to admit. The yellow dog of Peru is also known by other names: Romeo. Rainbow. Chorizo. He asks that his name never be mentioned through social media, Facebook in particular. He is measured and polite in this request but it is non-negotiable. The yellow dog of Peru may actually be an off-white colour. His tired, thin coat a bit rusted and patchy. I do not know why I am writing any of this.

November 29

And when will it be time to pen the dark again? Does the Peruvian birdsong make it easier or more difficult? What is it you are trying not to write? All the ways this light finds your sadness. The water down and down the steep slopes. Flowing and flowing and flowing.

November 30

"Why Peru?" asks the yellow dog. A generous opening for conversation. But I know the yellow dog is a sly dog. I know he already knows, "Why Peru?" My silence tells him that I know that he knows that I know. "Ah, the ceremonies," he says to encourage me. Yes, the ceremonies but it's too soon to trust a dog who barks at the drop of a hat and who takes his name from, among other things, a sausage.

December 1

Do we travel to understand that it's not necessary to leave? Or is it to bring home the few things we know for certain. Strip away the extraneous. The unimportant. For me, it's to know with great certainty that the love I hold for the two of you who wait at home is Everything and all that matters. Spin the compass needle. Fold and unfold the map. Smile through the Spanish you don't understand. Consider the contour lines of the map that curve and curve to create a topography of astonishment. Even at this altitude, the sickness is for home. Consider the certainty of love. And all that matters. Everything in Spanish. Understand travel as a translation of home. The two of you. For certain. Even at this altitude. A map of love folding and unfolding. Everything stripped away. The compass needle. The travel. Topography and all. The contours of love and a map of astonishment.

December 2

Sun-shower. Valley-wide. Cactus bloom. Mountainside. Watercolours getting wet. Everything bleeds before it sets. Tiny village far below. Stone terraces carved in rows. Inca ruins and satellites. Architecture. Dizzying heights. Cloud-shredding mountain peaks. White on blue in lengthening streaks. Valley floor. Mountain sky. Prayers pulled through the Shaman's eye.

December 3

Peruvian Haiku makes perfect sense in the Sacred Valley. Something about the manicured wildness of cross-hatched green fields carved and stepped into this ancient mountain valley invoke both the Haiku and the necessary contemplation required and inspired by the seeing.

Only in this light
A Peruvian haiku
Carved from ancient stone

Ollantaytambo
Climbing up into the sun
Worshipping the light

December 4

There is some sense of being drawn back up into the mouth of Cusco, everything happening in reverse. The plane that spit me out on to the tarmac just a short time ago is already waiting to pull me back up and away.

The road to Cusco.
In and out of poverty
And still all this light.

Waves of street peddlers
A waterfall of Spanish
No. Gracias. No.

December 5

Went for a storybook. Came back with a story. Wanted a happier ending but I'm not sorry. I'm not sorry for wanting more. Have not forgotten what I went there for.

December 6

Back to the world of brown and grey. Brown and grey through the middle of the day. Somber tableaux in fixed meter. Marsh grass death and swamp cedar. Back to the world of grey and brown. A grey-brown palette to bring you down. No sky. No sun. A tired quilt come undone.

December 7

Walking mantra in 4/4 time:
Breathing out — breathing in
In and in through love we spin
Breathing in — breathing out
Out and out all fear and doubt

December 8

Who is writing me now? I am not my journal entries. Easy to grow tired of being obtuse and cryptic in service of poetry and lyricism. Maintaining an historic vigilance against the possibility of eyes that pry not praise. Easy to tire of my attempts to self-impress. Side-tracked and worn down by my own epistemological concerns. Who is writing me now?

December 9

The prayer of being polished smooth. A stone or a spoon. Held in the palm of the hand. Utility and reverence. Please let this thin skin be polished so that inner and outer might meet in the presence of Grace. Water and wave. Wind and sun. Earth and stone and sand. Hold me up to the Light.

December 10

You travel afar in order to discover something that was always at home. And upon return you discover the map in a place where you couldn't help but find it.

December 11

Word upon word. That's how it's done. But today it seems no words are available. The journal sleeps. Dreamless. Dark. For now, maybe just move a few words back and forth. Adjust the furniture: a table beside the window for more light. An extra chair in case a visitor should arrive. The room just so. Any day now the words will return and we must be ready.

December 12

Nothing so mental as your health. Just you and your thoughts and thoughts and thoughts. Thinking and thinking and thinking: if only there weren't so many thoughts.

December 13

It's the middle of the month. Some are counting the days. Why and what we're counting is up for consideration. The number of shopping days left until Christmas? The number of days until the Saviour's arrival? The coming of Solstice? Counting the days up. Counting the days down.

December 14

Please, no gifts this year. Please, no gifts this year. Please, no gifts this year. Please, no gifts this year. Please, no gifts this year.

December 15

Insert seasonal poem here when the mood strikes.

December 16

The rain keeps everything green in its greyness. West coast impersonations down to a science here in the middle of the East. Day after day. Low clouds and mist. Even the Lake is Great in its greyness. The ferry boat cutting a line through the waves. No one getting out of their vehicles to bear witness to the fog and shroud. Just windshield wipers and Christmas carols sung slightly out of tune.

December 17

A classroom of kids and a world of back stories that would break your heart. Knowing only a dark hint of detail. Parents who don't know how. Bad decisions and birth marks. Cruelty and incompetence. The purest of innocence betrayed. And still the light the children bring to the world. *Peace on earth and mercy mild.*

December 18

Coffee cannot help you climb from this hole though it always feels like it just might. Still the view from the bottom is not without interest. The loss of perspective brings things in and out of focus. Like looking down the wrong end of the binoculars. Even the closest things feel far away. Even the trees for the forest.

December 19

The arrival of the *holidaze*. Trying to think outside the box of chocolates. Gift wrapped and counting calories. Surfing the shopping channel and feeling full of empty. There's no take home message in this kind of giving. Help us learn to give more fully. Less packaging. More heart. Less noise. More listening. Prepare us for the arrival.

December 20

Thank you for today. For the forest and for every tree in it. For the path that led me in and the path that brought me home. For the clouds and the occasional glimpses of pale sunlight that made the forest silver. Thank you for the noise of the chainsaw and the quiet afterwards and the many ways the woodstove will warm us in the days to come. Thank you for today.

December 21

Somewhere between the shortest day and the longest night we find ourselves looking inward for some other source of light. We light a fire. We light a candle. We mind the coals. We study the flame. We live in between. We feel the turning. We watch the sky come in off the lake. Watch the wood smoke curl and rise and mix with the pale sky and the light that is neither day nor night.

December 22

This is the time to listen closely for all the things that can and can't be heard. *Above thy deep and dreamless sleep the silent stars go by.* In the absence of light—songs and dreams and stories. *The hopes and fears of all the years are met in Thee tonight.*

December 23

Silent night. Everything unfolding according to some ancient script. *All is calm. All is bright.*

December 24

Stay close to family tonight. Everyone under the same roof. Coloured lights on the tree downstairs. A small bright star at the top. *Not a creature is stirring.* Even though all of us are years beyond squeals of delight — this truly matters. *Not even a mouse.*

December 25

Everyone is seeing green. No one even dreaming of a White Christmas this time round. It's not even on the radar. Not a second thought given. Out walking in the woods. Mild and welcoming. Clouds and sky and talk of a rare full moon tonight. Light filtering through the pines. Quiet thoughts. Then a commotion overheard. A confusion of crows. Over forty of them circling. Behaving oddly — even for crows. Flying this way then that. Gathering for the briefest of meetings in the highest branches of one great tree and then launching again. A chorus of complaints and the flapping of wings. Ragged and black in the Christmas sky.

December 26

There were good books to be found in every stocking along with the gift of time to dig in and enjoy them. Let us give praise and thanks for literature and let the reading begin.

December 27

Science tells us the light is now building. Building up to something more than it was yesterday. But it's far too early. Too early to say. Too early to tell.

December 28

I was hoping to take her to the blue café. Off the beaten track — slightly out of the way. Wish I might. Wish I may. Open my heart to her today. And hold her close at the blue café.

December 29

Forgotten radio days. Thankful for songs written in this key. Plain and ordinary 'home-on-the-range' kinds of songs. Folky and out of tune and full of charm. *Where seldom is heard a discouraging word. And the skies are not cloudy all day.*

December 30

The old year going out in a blaze of melancholy. This routine sadness that maps out uncertainty and finds us in the waiting room. All of us busy waiting. Waiting for our name to be called and hoping the news isn't as bad as we initially thought.

December 31

Should auld acquaintance be forgot. And never brought to mind? Walking the forest trail until there is no light left. The cabin that waits in the woods. Candles and a fire burning for all the friends who have shared this place in so many ways over so many years. *We'll take a cup of kindness yet for auld lang syne.*

January 1

The back roads are dry and center-bare as they used to say on the old road condition reports. Metallic light along the surface of the lake that December forgot to freeze over up here on The Shield. Stands of white pine always the best measure of any trip along this stretch. Great waving branches and these stretches of open winter water. A skiff of snow to suggest January has indeed arrived.

January 2

A pair of dice rolled out on the ice. Betting on your frozen heart. And the water below that flows and flows and sings its own song. With winter as a bridge to the chorus. And Al Purdy's 'Freezing Music' all cued up. Waiting and watching. Sevens, elevens and doubles. Roll them. Love and luck and the new year unfolding.

January 3

It's one foot then the other. One foot. Then the other. One foot. Then. The other. Onefootthentheoteronefootthentheotheronefoot thentheotheronefootthentheotheronefootthentheother. It's one foot then the other.

January 4

Right now I'm flatter than a pancake. Weaker than a handshake. Slushy like a milkshake. Blown out like a candle on a birthday cake. Tired but still awake. Knowing exactly what's at stake. Hoping for hope for God's sake.

January 5

Main Street: your home town. The main drag. Everywhere you look someone is limping. Some kind of awkward struggle witnessed by the bloodshot public eye. The sidewalks are brittle with old snow and ice. Poverty is a spectator sport that everyone attends and nobody watches. Some dirty blankets in a hollow doorway. We all avert our eyes. See everything.

January 6

The night is a tuning fork bounced off a metal roof. Concert pitch thrown all to hell by the clanging of so many instruments all trying to tune up in the crazy storm that's brewing. A symphony for climate change and fingerless gloves that's wreaking havoc on the wind instruments. The trombone section jocular despite ergonomic constraints. Temperature plummeting. The stars holding their breath. A flash freeze sure to be remembered well beyond tonight's performance. The conductor, still strung taut from the last storm, tests the air with his finger then touches the frozen fork with his tongue.

January 7

Please teach my pen to veer off the page and morph perhaps into crayon. And while I'm asking, please remove any and all lines that might dictate the flow of font or the splash of colour. Move me away from the literal and into the realm of wishful thinking. In addition, please free me from curricular conscriptions. Loosen expectation. Please let my pen know it's ok to go on ahead without me.

January 8

I can feel it coming in the air of night. Oh Lord. And I've been waiting for this moment for all my life. Oh Lord. It's not the first time this has happened. And according to the truth of cliché and the reality of shopping, it won't be the last. Trapped in the grocery store with Phil Collins following us down every aisle. We could wheel the cart faster. We could feign reading the product labels with greater care. But there is no escape. *Hello, I must be going.*

January 9

Traffic report: Moving at high speeds from two to four to eight to sixteen lanes in complete and utter anonymity. Navigating a public space under the shared pretense of privacy. Traffic building and building through heavy January rains. Remembering all those tire commercials claiming to eliminate hydroplaning. And here we are. Willing participants. Windshield wipers and Google maps. Believing that we know where we're going.

January 10

More and more he was less and less willing to go to the places that poetry was asking him to go. There were still all those things he needed to know. But the pages fell open like a diary and it was hard to trust what was actually being asked of him. Performative therapy always a possibility but the risk is to end up exposed and cheapened. Mid-sentence and feeling foolish for having tried to figure it out. Out loud on paper.

January 11

You continue to wake too soon to morning that is not morning. Black and cold beyond winter's window. A darkness inside. Remembering to breathe is only part of it. How to welcome in what you were hoping to keep out. Every fear you cannot name. Too late. Nothing to back your story now. Nothing to hold up to the light. Moving out on to the thin ice of words that may or may not hold your weight.

January 12

Message in a bottle: I'm here. Somewhere on shore. Need help. Can't explain in so many words.

January 13

Good omen today. Winter storm arrived. High winds. Big waves. Blowing snow. Choppy water the colour of winter. Water too cold to be water. Praying your way along the waterfront in a windstorm. Praying for the usuals: Strength. Courage. Patience. Humility. Love. Forgiveness. And a Sign of some sort. How to Let Go? A sign or a signpost. Wolfe Island is out there in the storm. Just off shore. Hunkered down and shouldering some of the load.

January 14

"Colour Me Happy." It's the new trend in bookstore sales. Why read a book when you can just colour one in? Colouring books for adults and everything Zen. And why not? These happy books now find themselves on prominent display beside all the best sellers. Another way to fend off sadness, negativity, fatigue and anxiety. Read or colour? Colour or read? The choice is yours. It's never too late for a happy childhood.

January 15

Do you have that friend in your life? The one who requires no explanations. Sees you through days you can't see yourself through. Tea on the stovetop. Wine on the windowsill. A little courage and some love to spare. Laughing and crying in equal measure. Muscled arms and a good grip on things. See her there now. An armload of wood for the stove and a shot of espresso to kickstart your courage.

January 16

Freezing rain and other forms of purgatory. A place between Here and There. Freezing rain. Cold but not cold enough. Adding layers of lacquer to the trees, to the cars, to the surface of the city. Adding unwanted weight to our memory of winter. Making a mockery of our ambulatory wishes. Walking with breath held. The circus high wire without drum roll or crowd noise. The laws of gravity given the day off. Slip sliding away.

January 17

No deeper than it has to be this morning. The lightest of snowflakes out the window. The kettle on. A good book for ballast. Drifting with someone else's story today.

January 18

Oh, but you *can* judge a book by its cover.

January 19

I never would have thought words could freeze like that—the window frosting over. The woodstove gone out. Nothing. Just dull thoughts scraped off the glass. Numb with worry.

January 20

They live somewhere nearby. Acrobatic and noisy. A bunch of black crows. Busy either making something happen or gathering themselves in clumps, restless spectators, taking in neighbourhood events. Just yesterday their keen sense for the unexpected was rewarded. Gathered in a tree, yelling at a red-tailed hawk that was busy killing a squirrel on the city sidewalk below. Jeering or cheering it was hard to tell. The hawk was focused on keeping its prey from leaving the scene. Blood on the snow. Flight seemed unlikely given the weight of the squirrel and its refusal to die. It was quite a show. A surreal urban scene. And it all made sense. A murder of crows calling out for more.

January 21

A lone pine tree in your front yard. It makes a little downtown forest for the wind to make music with in the branches that scatter light across the front of your house. Birds drop in. For conversation and for shelter.

January 22

22 below at the gas station. Big diesel tanker idling. The morning sun a hard yellow ball nobody wants to play with. Cars jockey. All of us slaves to polite pump instructions. *Please leave your card in the machine.* My tank filled in the time it takes to finish the Lord's Prayer. Car exhaust hovers. Toxic and meditative. I'm heading for a bigger blue of sky just a short skip north of here. The woods await. Thy Kingdom come. Thy Will be done. *Do you want your car washed today? Yes? No?*

January 23

The boy in the red t-shirt crossing the busy intersection. It's 20 below this morning with some wind chill to factor in. He might be 10 years old. He's heading for the donut shop on the far side of the street. Moving with purpose but not urgency. I try not to entertain all the possible scenarios my mind is wont to imagine about this boy and the story of the winter coat he is not wearing. He gives no indication that there is anything out of the ordinary about his morning routine. Car after car lefting and righting, moving on through the morning commute. Thinking about coffee, I turn left on a flashing green hoping he will have the sense to wait for the walking green. I look in my rear-view mirror for a last glimpse of the boy in the red t-shirt crossing the busy intersection.

January 24

Same spot. 4 days later. Not a crow in sight. The base of a huge neighbourhood maple. Just off the sidewalk. A squirrel lays prone in the snow. Very much dead. Very much frozen. Laid out neatly and anatomically save for its missing head. Same (dead) squirrel? The one the hawk attacked and was busy killing on his neighbourhood watch last week? Or different (dead) squirrel fallen prey to the same predator who has discovered a good thing and is working his beat efficiently and without fanfare? The crows aren't talking.

January 25

Just there on the horizon. A blood moon shrouded in cloud on the dark drive home. My daughter points it out as we sail down the highway together. The two of us talk. Then we don't talk. And it's just the three of us, my daughter, the moon and me.

January 26

The bus belches diesel and pulls into traffic sending a spray of grey slush in its wake. A steady rain sluices the streets and exposes the decaying snow banks and the dog shit and the rusted grocery cart. Let's try again tomorrow, shall we?

January 27

This is your Brain on January. Research, in dramatic fashion, continues to document the remarkable plasticity of the brain. Coffee tables now carry copies of 'The Brain that Changes Itself.' 'This is Your Brain on Music.' 'Brain on Fire.' 'Change Your Brain, Change Your Life.' It's common knowledge around the water cooler that the brain is always changing itself as experiences reorganize neural pathways. Despite being smarter about our brains, a well-meaning on-line link for brain plasticity — obviously for the hard-of-thinking — states, "As you know, the brain is not made of plastic." In fact, today my brain feels like a plastic Barbie doll with her head badly chewed by the family dog and left undignified, ass-up in the shit-brown snow bank. Barbie helps me write my new book: *This is Your Brain on January.*

January 28

So you finally became tired of being The Complete Perfectionist. Condolences and congratulations are in order.

January 29

It was Adrienne Rich who provided us with 'An Atlas of the Difficult World.' And here we are with our compass and a rough set of notes to go by. Best to leave no poem unturned.

January 30

You carry this gift. It makes you stumble. Makes you careless, mixed up, humble. A weight, a pulley, some stairs to climb. Never quite knowing what you're supposed to find. One false move and the spell is broken. The gift turned inward, never opened.

January 31

Caution: More Word Pairings. Hear say. Hot pants. Late comer. Line drive. Lost cause. Dim wit. Dog breath. Dive bomb. Bomb shell. Pile drive. Push over. Piss pot. Punk rock. Under tow. Over load. Wind up. Wet paint. Wild west. West wind. Zip drive. Rush hour. Road work. Road rage. Road rash. Off road. East coast. Easy pickings. Over board. Easy over. Over easy.

February 1

For these clouds. For this sky. For this late afternoon mid-winter light that stretches. For the sun that is becoming more and more insistent. For cracks in the sidewalk. For the two women walking on the other side of the street with their daughters. For the tiny bits of laughter they leave in their wake. For the feeling that pulls us all toward something brighter that is just around the corner.

February 2

God bless the 800-page novel (*The Goldfinch*) and the wordsmith (Donna Tartt) gifted with the art of drawing a line that pulls you up and out of yourself and into a world beyond anything you could ever imagine. Trade up this world for that world. Hers for yours. As though it could be otherwise.

February 3

Caffeinated clouds. Cancelled flights. Worried days. Windy nights. Cough drops. Call display. Won't be leaving here today. Cancelled clouds. Windy flights. Worried drops. Caffeinated nights. Heart space. On display. Couldn't leave here anyway.

February 4

You are exactly where you need to be. Hold hands with clichés like this. If you have a particular prayer for these kinds of situations best invoke it now. What kinds of situations? Neurotransmitter trouble. Synaptic misfirings. Mood disorders. Misgivings over hemispheric alignments. Concerns around amygdala function. Lost studies regarding the hippocampus. A generalized fear of fear. Hold on. You will get yourself back soon.

February 5

The game can only be played when water becomes ice. Some say, it's *the best game you can name.* Al Purdy's, *Freezing Music* providing the soundtrack to a constant carving and circling. For the most fortunate among us, there is a particular story encoded in the DNA. No thinking required. No thinking allowed. There are other requirements, of course, most provided by birthright: a predominance of fast-twitch fibers, voluminous lung capacity, certain biomechanical advantages. Brain and blood and bone arcing in an unlikely kinesiological triumph. Boys and men. Both. Together. Skill and will. Raw and transcendent. Something passed down. Flying close to the sun across a frozen surface.

February 6

A flat grey sky that wants to rain or snow. Snow or rain. A flat grey Sunday morning sky that casts the light of Amsterdam across this Southern Ontario streetscape. Architectural lines arthritic with history. European winter in my own backyard. No passport required.

February 7

Listen to Pema Chodron. She'll tell you: *Don't be swayed by external circumstances. Don't misinterpret. Don't vacillate. Train wholeheartedly. Don't wallow in self-pity. Don't be jealous. Don't be frivolous. Don't expect applause.*

February 8

The days go by February slow. A little more light. A lot more snow. February blues locked down tight. Pissing in the snowbank just for spite. Heard it's a leap year this time around. A month of Sundays come unwound. March comes in and turns on a dime. But February takes its own damn time.

February 9

I simply remember my favourite things. Wood smoke and woodstove warmth. The clean burn of beeswax candles. Fresh bread. Birdsong. Sun on snow. Starlight. Shots of espresso. Smoked salmon. Long walks. Late nights. Live music. Newly laundered sheets. Red wine. Dark chocolate. Driving through darkness. A novel newly opened. The next idea unfolding. *And then I don't feel so bad.*

February 10

I don't know where the words have gone. The words that issue forth with such great regularity when I ask them to. Never much cajoling involved. Mostly an invitation. I know it's a Gift but mostly I take it for granted. And now the place where the words come from seems to be sealed over. The days go by without words.

February 11

The moon hangs in the gap between our houses. Right there. Upside down just for show. More than a sliver. Less than what you originally paid for it. And so much more about the moon that can never be spoken without cliché and fear of reprisal: Moonshadow … The Man in the … The Dark Side of the … but, still, the moon is right there. In the gap between our houses. Right there. Your house. My house. The moon. Maybe we could share the cost of a frame. Open a neighbourhood gallery — call it 'Celestial Something or Other' — and leave it hanging right there.

February 12

Driving home under a blackness frozen over with stars. *And the radio plays that forgotten song.* It can't be any colder without something shattering. The landing gear locked up tight. Just your thoughts. Pitch black back roads and the demographics of loss and regret. How is it you've lived this long? The soundtrack spilling out behind you. The tiny fireworks of your tail-lights. The heart catalogued in song. But your friends. Oh, your friends. So much love. So much love. Driving home under a blackness frozen over with stars.

February 13

I went in broken looking for repair. More than a flat. Less than a spare. No, I really think there's something wrong. And I'm hoping I'm not already too far gone. Nothing I can point to. Nothing for sure. No disease without a cure. I keep thinking there's got to be a way. A pill or a plan at the end of the day. They said, 'We can't find anything wrong.' More than a cliché. Less like a song. I went in broken looking for repair. And a bit of healing. Can I meet you there?

February 14

Winter Storm Warning in Effect: A Personalized Weather Report
Hazardous winter conditions are expected. Snow, heavy at times, will taper off this evening. You may want to stay home with loved ones and bake cookies. *Total snowfall amounts of 25 to 40 cm are expected with this storm.* Brew a nice pot of tea. Maybe call an old friend. *Consider postponing non-essential travel until conditions improve. Rapidly accumulating snow will make travel difficult.* Red wine while gazing out the window. *Visibility may be suddenly reduced at times in heavy snow.* Curl up with a good book. Write a love note to someone in need of love. *A few hours of freezing rain or ice pellets near the St. Lawrence Valley is likely.* Curl up with your lover if you have one. Shovel only if you must. Perhaps ski or snowshoe downtown to witness how foolish and futile automobiles really are. *Please continue to monitor alerts and forecasts issued by Environment Canada.*

February 15

Literary escape. For all the writers who helped me read my way through several months of living that found me unable to brag about much. To bury oneself in a book. Hide between the covers. Throw oneself into a story. For all of the above. Books are beautiful things. Apologies for the many I just can't catalogue here.

The Night Stages. Three Views of Crystal Water. Carry Me Down. Goldfinch. All the Stars in the Heavens. A Spool of Blue Thread. When Breath Becomes Air. Alone in the Classroom. Gratitude. The Reserve. This is Happy. Euphoria. The Illegal. The Places That Scare You. How Music Works. The Sisters Brothers. Fifteen Dogs. Under the Visible Life. Jane Urquhart. Katherine Govier. M.J. Hyland. Donna Tartt. Adriana Trigiani. Anne Tyler. Paul Kalanithi. Elizabeth Hay. Oliver Sacks. Russell Banks. Camilla Gibb. Lilly King. Lawrence Hill. Pema Chodron. David Byrne. Patrick De Witt. André Alexis. Kim Echlin.

February 16

This pill leaves you staring into space. This pill comes in a designer case. This pill keeps the demons at bay. This pill makes you feel far away, then reverses the symptoms and brings you home. To a place where you never feel alone. Half the dose and it makes you sleepy. Double it up and it makes you weepy. Take this pill if you want to rest. One flew over the cuckoo's nest. Up and down and over the hills. Trying all kinds of little pills.

February 17

Sometimes words pull you right off the page into other worlds. You follow the feeling. You feel the feeling. The feeling follows you. Floating but not too high. With ballast enough to touch down here and there when needed. You've come to know and love these feelings and this kind of travel. You're visiting the place where songs live …

February 18

… Sometimes it's as simple as it seems. We are made for love. The heart knows exactly what it means because it's made for love. Yes, it's made for love. So you keep your heart as open as you can. Let love be your art. It's a feeling not a plan …

February 19

… And you find your heart will travel to a place it's never been. Like a lost thread it unravels into gold and blue and green. Let the pain and fear move through you. Let the love and light undo you. Because the heart is made for love …

February 20

… Sometimes it's not as simple as it seems. We're afraid of love. And the heart doesn't know exactly what it means. But it's still made for love. It's still made for love. Yet you close your heart. You don't want to feel the pain. Can't bear to fall apart from the feelings you can't name …

February 21

… And sometimes we don't listen to what the heart has in mind. It's easy to lose courage and the heart is hard to find. Let the pain and fear move through you. Let the love and light undo you. Because the heart is made for love. Yes, the heart is made for love.

February 22

There is a price to pay for living from the neck up. The view can be interesting from on high but the blood and guts stuff is usually what drives the ship. The captain has a plan but the crew does all the work. Some will always be busy asking, 'How does it work?' while others will always be busy making it work.

February 23

Freezing Rain Warning in Effect: The Forest for the Trees:
A freezing rain advisory means that periods of freezing rain or freezing drizzle will form a glaze on roads resulting in hazardous travel. The birch trees seem to take it the worst. Huddled together along the roadsides. Iced branches bent over in prayer. Resignation and redemption. Both up for grabs. *Conditions rapidly deteriorating. Power lines may also be brought down due to ice accumulation.* Somehow it's safety in numbers for the sugar maples. They've probably seen worse. The sugar bush has always had a certain solidarity to it. The maples have been to the party and membership has its privileges. *Travelers should be prepared to alter plans accordingly as driving conditions are likely to deteriorate significantly this evening and continue into tomorrow morning.* 'Bring it on,' say the black spruce. Tough talk from a tough bunch of trees. *Please continue to monitor alerts and forecasts issued by Environment Canada.*

February 24

Next day. Post storm. Driving north beyond the city limits. Iced trees against the brilliant blue of morning sky and a great silence. Dazzling. Yes, dazzling. Sunlight and ice. Entire forests that look like someone put a finger in a socket. The normally stodgy ironwoods appear over-dressed for a party. Beautiful and glittery. Just a touch over the top. Beech, shimmery, shivering and a bit awkward with so many of last year's leaves still pasted on. And the birch. The birch suffer in silence. The white pine not much better off. Such a beautiful and cruel magic here in this place where it can rain ice.

February 25

A group of toddlers let loose in the library. See them there among the stacks of books. A playgroup dispersing, parent-less in the brief instant it takes for the librarian to turn the last page. Noise and clammer. The signal for parents to Return to Duty. Parents who had taken temporary leave to wander the stacks into other worlds. Parents looking for Fictional Escape or Financial Freedom. Parents looking for Life beyond Parenting. Parents looking for Parenting Made Easy: 'Yoga for In-between Feedings.' 'Healthy Meals for Families on the Go.' Now it's back to board books. Books that forever hold us in between durable covers that withstand tears, tantrums, drool and unanswerable questions. *Guess How Much I Love You?* Turn the page and we'll see.

February 26

Meantime, Dr. Seuss, who likely knows and cares very little for the micro-management of family life, still holds court in the Children's Area. Timeless and ageless, he offers up story after story for parent and child. *On Beyond Zebra! Horton Hatches the Egg. Yertle the Turtle and Other Stories.* Dr. Seuss and his impeccable timing. Once you get started it's hard to stop rhyming. Spent the next couple of days matching lines with Dr. Seuss ...

February 27

… *Step with great care and great tact. And remember that life's a great balancing act.* Splash out some fiction to go with your fact. Remember loosely, let go of exact …

February 28

… *If things start happening, don't worry, don't stew. Just go right along and you'll start happening too.* Dr. Seuss, I presume, with stories like songs that go Zip and go Zoom. Known by few as Theodor Geisel. On horseback, by mule, unleaded and diesel. Delivering wisdom in bits and pieces. Perfect distraction while writing your thesis.

February 29

From Seuss to Rumi. Not such a stretch, really: *When a man makes up a story for his child/He becomes a father and a child together, listening.* And who else to listen to but Rumi? In the book that is not a book. Of spells. Of sorrows. Of scriptures. Ecstasy. Mystical conundrums. Unfathomable love. Poems. Prayers. Wisdoms. Cosmic Humour. Lithe Metaphor. All before afternoon coffee break. And now my own child has traveled 18 times around the sun for good measure. And many more round the kitchen table. Chasing our tails and then waiting in hopes of catching ourselves coming round again. Birth and death recognizing one another from time to time. My image growing smaller with every turn.

March 1

March comes in like the lion you once drew in the 2nd Grade. Mostly mane. Wild and gold and unruly. Spindly lion legs assigned to support a grand, over-sized lion head. Paper roar and a spiky sun, up high in the top right hand corner of the page. Enough golden light to know we'll go out like a lamb.

March 2

Bright Wednesday morning wishes. Just a hint of new snow and the Serenity Prayer. The same walk made new by what we know will soon arrive. Same sun. Different angle. New possibilities. *And the wisdom to know the difference.*

March 3

Who can I write to today? What invitation? What details? Looking down the list. So many who could use a kind word. You, perhaps? Are you still there if I don't write? Well, no matter. I love you. You've given me so much for such a long, long time. Remember walking along the high ridge of desert mesa together? The moon came around the corner, full as full could ever be. And the tiny white night flowers that bloomed in the sand right before our eyes? Surely this happened if we both witnessed it together. Here's a sketch I've included of us holding hands. I know things were rough for a while there. You've turned it around again though. I'm so glad. I'm adding some mandolin and a bit of banjo in this paragraph. Just for fun. I hear you smiling. Thanks for being there dear friend. I'm closing with a tuba solo just because.

March 4

There were surprise skaters on the lake today. Not just any lake. It was the Big Lake: Ontario. It seemed a confusion of seasons: the sun putting on a sparkly show, a bunch of birds talking up Spring on my walk home and people out there walking on a frozen lake.

March 5

There is something new waiting for you. What is it? It most likely won't come in the form you expect or hope for. It might not be at the grocery store. It could be a person, place or thing. Something in the neighbourhood? Maybe. It won't be by chance. The lottery numbers rarely line up. There's a song playing in your head. Some words to go with the music. It seems that it's always the smallest of birds that take the biggest of risks.

March 6

Families on Sunday mornings. Up early. Sleeping in. Looking ahead. Looking back. Bacon and eggs. Jam on toast. The newspaper. The dog waiting to walk the first person up. Cartoons left over from Saturday mornings. Coffee. Arguments. Procrastination. Snow on the roof. Rain against the windows. Sunlight in the kitchen. Worship. More coffee. A tabby curled up on an old abandoned housecoat. And, of course, television: BaseballFootballGolfBasketball. The obligatory chores. Jogging. Napping. Homework. Melancholy. More and more space taken up with thoughts of Monday morning and the upcoming week that begins to press in on families on Sunday evenings.

March 7

Luck is right where you left it last Fall before the snows arrived. In the backyard. Just off the deck where you love to watch the night sky tilt and tilt until your head is full of stars and it's time to come inside and ready yourself for bed. Luck—the shiny coin showing through the melting snow. Luck—the last row of stacked wood that will warm you until it's time to throw open the windows. Luck—the laughter coming from over the fence, now that people are slowly beginning to venture outside. Luck that saw you through another winter. As luck would have it, in the backyard watching the night sky tilt and tilt and tilt. Thanking your lucky stars.

March 8

The heavens are shifting ever-so-slightly. The constellations hanging in a different place than when you last took the time to look up. There's no science involved. Not a telescope in sight. Just the naked eye noticing. Taurus. Perseus. Canis Major. There's talk among the stars. And we all know Orion is unable to keep a secret: winter is losing its grip.

March 9

What can the crow teach us about Spring? I don't know, but in the time it took to watch him oddballing around in the branches up high, a noticeable amount of snow seemed to have disappeared from the snow banks below. Not possible I hear you saying. And a reasonable response it would be. But don't tell the crow that. He'll only point out all the other impossible things he's already made happen today. The semiotics seminar he conducted this morning. The flight lessons he convinced the local squirrels to sign up for. His ability to stop traffic with minimal effort. These and other things: talking backwards while flying upside down, turning Winter to Spring with a crooked beak and just the ragged feathers on his back.

March 10

A bit of patience and a touch of restraint and you wouldn't have had to *photoshop* that cardinal into your latest work, "My Backyard in Mid-March." Understandable given the grey splotches of snow retreating across the lawn and the skeletal trees still far from imagining themselves any kind of green. The rusted bicycle leaning against the falling-down fence. You can't be blamed for wanting to paintball a bright red bird in the foreground given everything you've been through. Months and months now since they drained the colour from the scene. But it's all coming back. Not today. Not tomorrow. Not next week. But a bit of patience and a touch of restraint can go a long, long way.

March 11

Let the days keep coming. Count them in whatever ways you can. In whatever ways you might wish. Dream, even. Let the days keep coming. Let there be no secrets. Each of us has been keeping something like faith. Each and every day. Let the days keep coming. As Mr. Paul Simon once sang, *It's not just me and it's not just you, this is all around the world.*

March 12

Sunrise 7:15 AM   Sunset: 7:12 PM

Spring ahead. A confusing time for many. An hour lost in the dark while we sleep, then wake to the same light only different. A confusion of time. Some insist it's more like a practical joke we play on ourselves every year. In these digitized days in which we live, there aren't even that many clocks to 'spring ahead.' Gone are the days we get to play god with the hands of the clock on Sunday morning. But there is no confusion around the way moods lighten once everything is held in place by the hands of time newly turned. Daylight is, in fact, well worth saving. All hands now point to the sign: Spring Ahead.

March 13

The forest begins to shadow and darken. Backlit as the evening comes on. Crescent moon. Silent meadow. The pond below still frozen over. Not a soul here to tell but you.

March 14

Just beside the icy stream. The sugar shack is full of steam. A maple syrup maker's dream. A gift to drizzle on ice cream.

March 15

Both of you were born on this day. A father. A son. 80 years apart. My father: 1918. My son: 1998. One birth made it possible for me to become a son. One birth made it possible for me to become a father. Father and Son. One now long gone, the other just getting going. And me, both and somewhere in between.

March 16

Don't wait for me. You've got it going on. You're already hearing things well beyond my range. Eyes open to all that's possible. Sure-footed. Fired by youth. And me? I'm right behind you but I stop more often. Distracted by the view and by the thought of how different our worlds.

March 17

Birdsong is back in the neighbourhood. In backyards and hedges, telephone wires and treetops. There is a growing chorus that crowds out the chickadee: grackles, wrens, sparrows. There's a cardinal a few fences over that easily outstrips the general chatter. Listen for it. Not lacking in confidence, the cardinal auditions, not just for any part in the show. Only the lead will do. And according to cardinal logic, there's no way in hell a robin's going to get the part. The birds are back. Acknowledgements and thanks to the chickadees for minding the store when no one else wanted the job.

March 18

A bit more about birds. I think most would agree: there's always room for a seagull or 2 by the water's edge. Picture them there now. Floating high above the water. Include a boat, preferably a sturdy vessel cutting through the waves. Add a strong offshore breeze and add appropriate sound effects. This is *not* the scene I'm picturing. It's more like concrete urban-ugly, the streetscape bleak and bare and not quite thawed out yet. Seagulls have been showing up in parking lots and back alleys like bad B-movie actors. Squawking. Bickering, too. Splitting hairs. Guffawing. Laughing their heads off at a joke they don't want us in on. Mocking and mean-spirited. Dirty-beaked. Just listen to them go on and on about what you can do with your sailboat and where you can stick summer.

March 19

Today is the day to gather up everything the forest discarded over the long winter season. Today is the day to gather up everything and set it ablaze in the stone fire pit behind the cabin. The flames have held their tongue through these long, hard months. Licking the hearth, firing the furnace. Solemn and fierce. Today is the day the fire burns for *nothing in particular and everything in between.* Sun and cloud and wisps of smoke through the upper reaches of the hardwoods. Blue sky and more. Staring at the flames. Sparks sail skyward. A ritual of fire that makes room for everything that follows in this season of seasons. A forest meditation. A careful listening. A quiet prayer. Today is the day.

March 20

Each of us move, slowly at first, in our own ways. Out of winter and into a light that is made up mostly of memory. Into a light that changes everything. Absent for so long. Now it is upon us. This light. Clear and harsh. Showing us all those things we forgot we missed seeing. Can we ever be ready for all this seeing? Nothing and nothing and nothing and then: Here. The light. Clear and harsh as we blink ourselves out of hibernation.

March 21

Tell me more about typewriter love. How your fingers find the keys in the dark. Eyes closed. Wish upon wish coming true. How the carriage return signals the end of one beautiful thing and the beginning of another. How the font bleeds ever so slightly on to the page as you strike the keys. A memo. A love letter. A tattoo. How the absence of spell check liberates you. Frees you to err on the side of a permanence that is reckless and unguarded. A clatter of metal keys that sometimes tangle in their rush to say everything and more.

March 22

This is not a day for asking questions, not a day on any calendar. Ah, to be so blessed as to follow Rumi, shimmering, through the world he paints, the poems he sings that arrive in a gift of notes. Words dissolving on the tongue. Silence along the riverbank. Deep canyons filled to the brim with every kind of blue. Shadow and light. Forever delighted by missed understanding. *The rest of this poem is too blurry for them to read.*

March 23

If you can't think of anything good to say, don't say anything. Maybe best to check back tomorrow.

March 24

Memory # 318: 24 years old. 24. That's how many trips you'd managed to make around the sun to that point. So many summers gone by since. It might have been your first Trans Canada pilgrimage. Small enough to disappear standing on the side of the highway. Swallowed up by mountains. Your heart bursting over Rogers Pass. It was East to West that time. A solo trip. The tree line steep and jagged enough to knock words loose and send them careening down the cut lines. An avalanche of poetry that would never even make it as far as Revelstoke. No matter. *24 and there's so much more.*

March 25

Breathe deeply on this day. It won't come again. In and out. Everything moving through you. In and out.

March 26

Our children are copper cliffs and silver blue. Part of them me, part of them you. One in September, a whisper of Fall. She is the market flower stall. The other child, a gift for Spring. March's tiny offering. Not yours. Not mine. Loving the beautiful ties that bind.

March 27

Witnessing a lake lose its ice is nothing like watching paint dry. In fact, it's nothing short of witnessing a miracle. So much that can't be seen. Imagine the science. A lot of time spent staring. Not staring. Thinking. Not thinking. Sitting at the shoreline you can hear the sun at work. Listen: ice and water renegotiating the terms of their relationship. Some restless clouds overhead. The forest on the far shore. A local kingfisher back in business. Blue reminding itself just how wide a palette it wields. And all that magic at work just below the surface.

March 28

What to do with this routine sadness? Too many songs already written. Too much cliché when you risk mixing sad with lonely. Too much of yourself to face. Say a prayer for friends who aren't afraid to hold you. Love you. Light a fire in the stove for you as the day darkens and the rain comes on. Sit with you for as long as it takes.

March 29

It's only here in the darkened theatre that you're life is filled with light. People getting up to leave as the credits roll. None of us wanting to claim loneliness as our very own. Just as long as you're not too scared to feel. No one will give up on you if you don't give up on yourself. You can always take this short story and make it long. We know you're good for it. You'll find your way through.

March 30

Today's news is World War II with 'better' coverage. Bombs tearing us apart in high definition. It's 24 hours. All bleak, all the time. Dark and darker still. The War on Terror. The Terror of War. Drone strikes and a twitter feed. Refugee reports and people's lives ripped apart in real time. The first worlders making sure their own news is Facebook-worthy. Someone please show me how to write poetry again.

March 31

March goes out. Neither lion nor lamb though, on this day, both creatures would no doubt prefer someplace much drier. Heavy rains all day long. One would almost be forgiven for using 'miserable' as a descriptor for this dark chill that is neither winter nor spring, lamb nor lion. Just March going out.

April 1

Lucky enough to look up and see a pileated woodpecker cut through the clearing up ahead. Undulating flight. Crazy flash of red. Turkey vultures, newly returned, already a ubiquitous presence overhead. Nuthatches, too. Shy and comical. Upside down on the trunk of a big oak along the path. And, of course, you always hear them before you see them: a pair of hawks somewhere nearby. Fingers crossed for a sighting. More luck: a red-tail drifts over the meadow on unseen currents that pull us all forward into Spring.

April 2

Driving the back roads in the small, unclaimed hours of the night after rehearsals and gigs. Running on headlight faith and a psychedelic soundtrack that narrows the road and pulls the forest in close as breath. Clouds stir the moon. The end of each trip signaled only by the upstairs sounds of your children sleeping.

April 3

Poet Mark Nepo says, *song is not a luxury but a necessary way of being in the world.* These words have a way of making me unafraid to start in again today. There's serious work to be done.

April 4

An impatient crow alarmclocks its way through the dull grey woods. *Wake up now! Wake up now! Now! Now! Now!* Everything still dormant beneath its black wings. *Surely you can't expect me to do this on my own?!* You stop to witness its ragged flight through the matchstick trees. The forest path a soggy, somber welcome mat. Though its black cloak seems an unlikely harbinger of Spring, you can still appreciate the shape shifter's frustration. Can feel your own sense of betrayal in Spring's annual promise of 'any day now.'

April 5

Today, driving north of town where there are more trees and lakes than buildings and people, a bald eagle flies overhead going east to west. I crane my neck, looking and looking and looking, hoping to make the moment last. Hoping not to crash the car.

April 6

Lost lyrics always looking for a song. Lyrics—always showing up when they're least expected. Lyrics—always begging for a melody. Lyrics—always some assembly required:

Someone's stacking wood. Someone steals a car.
Someone's feeling good. Sitting at the bar.

Someone knocks on wood. Someone else is lost.
Someone falls in love no matter what it costs.

Someone sings a song. Someone steals a kiss.
With love and poetry, it's sometimes hit and miss.

April 7

Pay phone booth and a parking meter. Old poster of a vaudeville theatre. Morning sun. Evening news. The ones who never get to choose. A bunch of children holding hands. A line up at the taxi stand. Nothing as formal as an evening gown. I think this might be your hometown.

April 8

You can no longer walk by without looking. You never used to look. There were always lots of other possibilities to distract you on your walk home: the wind in the trees, dog walkers, kids on bikes, various local characters carrying on animated conversations with themselves. But it's a foregone conclusion now. You can no longer walk by without looking. Look, there it is now: the little lottery sandwich board out front of the corner store advertising the current jackpot total: 44 MILLION. The lottery numbers tumble out and line up in your mind. Send you high above the neighbourhood. Looking down at yourself looking down at the sign. Thinking of all the combinations and permutations. All the beautiful complications. 44 million reasons for not stopping at the store. Just looking.

April 9

The heart knows the wandering path that climbs up through the cedars. The mind counts the steps and the years and remembers beauty gathered along the way. Today there are glimpses of blue beyond green beginning to appear. Cedars that invite rare and limited offerings of open pond and marsh. Views seen only at this time of year. This no-longer-Winter, this almost-Spring, this not-yet-Summer time of year.

April 10

I was desperately unhappy trying to adjust to the world. Carrying these words of Alfred Wellington Purdy with me on this gunmetal sky day. The world falling grey and flat and heavy at my feet. The walk, slow. Uphill. There is snow mixed with hail and high winds on this Spring day. I might make an attempt at scraping together a poem out of the slush but Al has already walked this walk. Instead, I crack open one of Mr. Purdy's poems like a beer — a bottle of Labatt's 50 — while Al lights an unfiltered Export A and tells it like it is.

April 11

If the flow of poetry were ever to cease, let me tell you both now: my love for the two of you is always and forever the poem I'm working on. Always the next line waiting in the wings. Fired by love and love only.

April 12

Some days the music is just not there. You can't find a song anywhere. Just a bunch of notes floating beyond your out-of-tune listening. What to do? Listen. Listen again. Listen some more. Hear that? Turns out you were trying too hard. It's not a test. Music moves as it must. As guitar pioneer Les Paul reminds us: *One note can go a long way if it's the right one.*

April 13

Metaphors mentioning the moon have no effect on the moon. And who would ever argue with Rumi? Even so, there can be no denying the moon's long history with those who cannot help but build a ladder to the stars to get a better look. The moon's better half never full of itself.

April 14

I guess you know by now that you're going to keep writing these poems even though they will never pay the rent. They won't even pay for your coffee bill but who's counting? Spare change. And a change is as good as a rest and put the rest on my tab. And tab key your way across the page until a carriage return is required. Your mind *does* go quiet every now and then. Blessed relief written all over you. Just that moment or two is enough for the whole world to appear on your front porch. There's no accounting for loss. Spellcheck Discount coupons honoured here.

April 15

You want to be understood. You've told the publisher: no author photo on the dust jacket. Under no circumstances. And no TED Talks either. A small publicity tour to small groovy towns only. It's just that this Gift … it comes with no instruction manual. And skipping your way through childhood meant that things that might have been easy no longer are. How hard can it be? Don't answer that …

April 16

… Or if you do, make sure you get your dissertation committee's approval in triplicate. It could have been simple at one time but complexity theory has taken over the entire block. Pill bottles with fine print. Sign up here for the Side Effects Seminar. You know there's something so pure and beautiful playing on the radio somewhere. And Love. That's what the next song is for. You just want someone to know.

April 17

The UV Index makes its triumphant return to our lives today. A human metric designed to inform us of the length of time it will take for ultraviolet rays to damage exposed skin. A warning, yes, but also an invitation in quiet moments like this to tilt our faces upwards toward the sun. Eyes closed. Not yet thinking of summer heat that will surely find us looking for shade. For now, we are simply phototropic creatures turning toward the light. Think crocus, not sunflower. Think microclimate not meadow. Opening. Slowly opening.

April 18

Mid-morning light and a sonata for tree branch and birdsong. A backyard world unfolding. A lovely ensemble. Not technically demanding enough for Debussy perhaps but Brahms would no doubt be pleased by the play of shadow and light.

April 19

Somewhere along the line you seem to have forgotten that manual labour is what's required to get the job done. Even the magnetic poetry kit you got for the fridge requires some assembly. Maybe you've been looking in the wrong places. The Muse does not take holidays. Nor does she punch the time clock just because you started your shift. Be prepared to throw it all away and start again.

April 20

Just a guitar and a few songs. And a bunch of children who offer up love and trust despite the many ways that each of these precious gifts seem to have in some way been withheld from them. How do they do it? And what else to do now but sing together — something in a major key that makes us all giggle.

April 21

Morning sun angling off the water. Split rail fence along the roadside. Yellowed marsh grass and last year's broken down cattails. And there they are: 2 red-winged blackbirds who make it official: Full Spring Ahead.

April 22

Unofficial Spring Proclamation: To the attention of all poets, hikers, bikers, joggers, bloggers, walkers, talkers, naturalists and artists of all stripes. Let it be known that from this day forward the following words and phrases will once again be reissued and reinstated into the lexicon: 'dappled sunlight,' 'babbling brook,' 'light breeze,' 'sun-warmed,' 'greenery,' 'earthen,' 'canopy,' and 'forest floor.' After much deliberating, the sub-committee overseeing clichés has seen fit to approve and authorize all of the above as witnessed here on this 22nd day of April in this sun-dappled forest by God, 3 turkey vultures, 1 nuthatch, 2 deer mice and a solitary crow who, like last year, will likely ignore and/or boycott any and all proclamations, unofficial or otherwise.

April 23

Spring is a lesson in remembering. How is it that green finds us here once again? Is it only a trick of the light that loosens winter's coil? What a long, long trip around the sun it's been. And now these seedpods swell. Buds waiting to burst. The days are saplings. Shy, gentle, bending. The light making up for lost time.

April 24

Praying for the necessary healing. Surrendering to each little feeling I'm feeling. Scattered light bounces off the ceiling. Praying for the necessary healing.

April 25

Cold rain is rain just the same. Some of us watch from the windows wishing for something other than what we are experiencing right now. Discouraged, some of us want only warmth and more warmth. We want Spring's curve to be predictable. Blue and more blue. Green and more green. Warm and warmer. No steps back, please. Some of us watch from an open field with faith planted firmly in the soil. Accepting what is. Patience is what draws April into May.

April 26

Waiting for someone to put the blue back in your sky? Just for today? Someone to banish any and all greys that might insist on being part of the package? Friends and loved ones have been known to conjure up certain spells, magic and otherwise, for just this kind of situation. Step outside right now. Look around. Indeed, you are loved.

April 27

Children hold sharpened sticks around the fire. Make brave connections between the smoke that swirls around their faces, the small hands that grip the wood, and the marshmallows their parents have oh-so patiently applied like bait. Plump little clouds, white and bobbing, somewhere between disaster and delicious reward. So much to be said about the difference between the open flame and glowing coals.

April 28

Sharp as a tack. No stranger to a hammer and nail. Power tools if that's what the job requires. You are a songbird with a falcon's sense of timing. An eye for each and every detail. Living there by the ocean. Most at home in your garden. Roots and wings. No job too big or too small. Well-travelled. And the immaculate care you've taken to show us ourselves. All these years. Year after year after year. Uncompromising. Nails on a chalkboard. Fingering a silk gown. A lifelong commitment to the way of words. Not this or that. But this *and* that. Every poem a story of how a life might be lived with courage and a fierceness for the telling. Made us cry when we expected a good laugh. Unafraid of a good guffaw. Deeper and deeper you go. Thank you, Lorna. Thank you.

April 29

Today's sky. A blue dome streaked with wisps of clouds that whisper, "Lie down. Right over there in that little patch of green." I seem to be the only one who hears the invitation. Everyone else is busy being busy. Taxi cabs, tow trucks, tractor trailers. All tuned in to the concrete hum. The little patch of green seems like the safest and most sane option. The light and more. Spirituality and particle physics and a blue big enough to convince even the skeptics to sign up for the seminar.

April 30

It's time to get out of town. No one chasing you but your own shadow. It's time to get out of town. Nothing slowing you down.

May 1

A man in a wheel chair smokes a cigarette on the platform of the station at Chatham. Doesn't look up as we stop to let some passengers off while other passengers board. He looks like he's not waiting for anybody or anything. He's not coming or going. The train pulls away slowly. Everyone leaves something behind. Carrying their baggage with them.

May 2

From the train: farmers' fields. Field after field. Brown stubble. Dark earth ready to receive. Stands of trees. Muddy riverbeds. Backyards. From the train: sand and gravel. Scrap metal and abandoned machinery. Concrete abutments. Steep berms dropping down to the tracks. From the train: more farmers' fields. Fields. Fields. Fields. And the optical illusion created by fresh new lines of green running perpendicular to the train that clicks by, sleight of hand, like a card trick. From the train: tracks over trestles. Freight trains and other ghosts. All witnessed from the train rolling out and out. On and on.

May 3

Life is short so go slow. Life is short and don't you know — you can try to hold time keep it close to your heart. Try to paint every dream that you dreamed from the start. But the colours will bleed and the images run. Leave you holding your breath chasing after the sun. Life is short so go slow ...

May 4

… What matters most is open to persuasion. What matter most is up for debate. What matters most comes down to the occasion. What matters most lives between faith and fate. So go real slow. Go the way you've been wanting to go. You never know but fast may not be better than slow …

May 5

… Life is short so go slow. Life is short and don't you know — that the colours fly by but they swing round again. So try to forget to keep remembering. Let go of time and stay close to your heart. Let the days come together let the days come apart. Life is short so go slow.

May 6

There you are in a vehicle. In the passenger seat headed out of town toward Spring. Moving at a good fast clip. Your only job is to roll down the window and witness the landscape flying by. If you scrunch your eyes together just so, everything becomes a happy blur of green. Not just any green. But every green. All greens. Dizzy with green. Green with everything but envy. The palette so full of green: Kelly green. Laurel green. Lime green. Lawn green. Olive green. Pistachio. Artichoke. Asparagus. Avocado. Apple green. Brunswick green. Castleton green. Chartreuse. Sea green. Shamrock green. Spring green. Emerald green. Fern Green. Forest green. Moss green. Mint green. Pigment green. Pine green. There you are inside Spring. And if you scrunch your eyes together just so …

May 7

Through a glass darkly. Half-empty to boot. This can't be the way May is supposed to begin. What happened to yesterday's feelings? So light and light-hearted? How could things turn that hard and fast?

May 8

In off the road. A weary unloading of your bags. Check in. The hotel that is Every Hotel. The lobby. The front desk. The ice machine. The hallway's heavy carpets. The generic artwork. Holding your breath. Holding your key. Searching for the matching room number. Pretending that this hotel is not every other hotel. Wanting simply to open the door and disappear behind it. Imagining that this room is waiting for you and you only. A chocolate on your pillow would be icing on the cake.

May 9

Parenting does not get easier. Parenting does not get harder. Parenting gets both easier *and* harder but mostly it just gets different. As they grow older, our children are no longer our children. And yet the lifeline that runs through our lives will forever bind us as parent and child. Babies need every available ounce of love we can give them. They also need to be fed and diapered. Happy toddlers need someone to affirm and celebrate and share their joy. Happy toddlers need to be held. Tantruming toddlers need a space to release some innate rage that lives inside them. Tantruming toddlers need to be held. In the moment it takes to turn our heads, our toddlers are teenagers who want to borrow the car. Our teenagers want to travel overseas. Our teenagers want to go to parties. Want to experiment with alcohol, with drugs, with gender, with their sexuality. Problems and difficulties can no longer be solved by holding our teenagers. This can feel very problematic. But make no mistake, our teenagers needs to be held.

May 10

Lake Ontario comes in waves today. Whitecaps confirm what our Grade 6 Geography textbook told us: The Great Lakes are inland oceans. Far as the eye can see.

May 11

Smart phones don't make us smarter. I'm just thinking out loud, here. Going out on a bit of limb. An un-researched opinion based on anecdotal observations: that woman walking down the street having an animated conversation. Only a shade different than talking to herself, really. The teenager oblivious to everything but the screen he swipes at. The father walking his children to school. Perhaps he's checking a bit of email before he gets to work. Checking in as he checks out. Everyone staring at their phones. No one notices the clouds clotheslining across the tops of the buildings downtown. No one notices how in love that couple are who wait at the bus stop. Everyone is texting and tweeting. Tweeting and texting. Updating their photo on Facebook. Or maybe they're listening to an intellectually stimulating podcast? Maybe watching an insightful documentary? Or perhaps they're writing little poems on little screens.

May 12

Perhaps there is someone somewhere who could gather all of this light into a poem. The silk gown of early evening, translucent now. The burden lifted from the shoulders of day. Perhaps there is someone somewhere who could gather this poem into light. Light that has come such a long, long way to be here. Now.

May 13

We're still hoping to fast food our way out of our problems. A burger and fries to bury doubt and discomfort. Wash it all down until we're full with empty calories. The junk we call food. The life we call living. Nothing we can't drive thru. Shame and blame. Left turn lanes and longing for something we can't quite name. Something better than here and now.

May 14

Once May gets June in its sights there's no turning back. Don't even think about it. April showers were acknowledged and appreciated but May now has other ideas. Postcard clouds appear as previously advertised: white and puffy. Lilacs along the roadside make rolling down the car windows mandatory. Weather most promising. Wish you were here.

May 15

Over at the meadow's edge, something bright catches my eye. It's a brilliant yellow flower and it's flying toward the forest. It couldn't have chosen a better time to burst into bloom. A tiny piece of joy in flight. A well-meaning friend tells me it was likely an American goldfinch or a Canada warbler, or possibly even a vireo. While he is busy studying the bird guide, I catch a last glimpse of the tiny flower disappearing into a garden of trees.

May 16

Road kill, Part 1. Today's drive north into the Canadian Shield cries out for a different spin on Spring's Rite of Passage. Why did the porcupine cross the road? Same reason the raccoon, the deer, the squirrel, the snake, the skunk, the frog and so many others did. We built a road right through the middle of their natural habitat and these animals are heading home. Or leaving home. Or looking for food or possibly a mate. The passage is fraught with peril. Particularly in Spring. Deer in the headlights? You bet. Or broad daylight. Full speed ahead. They don't stand a chance.

May 17

Road kill, Part 2. Full speed ahead and staring at the remains of what we've left in our wake. Sometimes slowing down or swerving slightly to avoid running over the crushed mass that lies on the road. Entrails. Lots of entrails. Sometimes we recognize the road kill. Sometimes a raccoon looks like it's taking a little nap by the side of the road. Other times, it's anybody's guess. Blood and guts. Porcupines just aren't meant to build up speed for these kinds of crossings. Quills at all angles from a pulpy mass in the middle of the road. Crows and vultures playing chicken with cars. The brave ones tear at the flesh and hop away just in time to avoid becoming road kill themselves. Spring's Rite of Passage.

May 18

The lawn mower season has officially begun. And no birds sang.

May 19

Sometimes we're not in charge of the music. Neighbours have other ideas. Grunge not necessarily your cup of Sonatina. Acid folk in E minor. Opus no. 27. The sun stretches the day to fit all sizes. Blue sky coming down over our heads. Some have left town. A flower there. Concrete make-over. May rips up the pavement and February is forgotten. Grace and Goodness here with us right now.

May 20

Friends tip us over into Spring. Three yellow tulips stick their necks out. Green finds new ways to surprise. It's all imagery. Metaphors are lost in translation. May falls in your lap. A gift from March and April. What can you do? Accept. Yes is the only answer. Poets refuse to fill the forms out in triplicate. Music fills in the spaces. Love the notes. Really love them. The acoustics are great in here.

May 21

Just like this. Just like that. The words must come forth. On demand. In time. No rhyme scheme required. Just words to ease the worried mind. Coffee always a measure used to go by. To get by. If there weren't words? Hieroglyphs, I suppose. Cave paintings maybe. Yoga. Mud and clay. Pushups. A dance routine. Water colour. Talk therapy. Mind games. Aquafit, perhaps.

May 22

Today: looking for new ways to present green as the most brilliant feature on Spring's canvas. Mix it with a cityscape: buildings, streets, concrete, glass and it's still green. It's still about the light. Still about the voice that persists.

May 23

Rain and sun. A good mix. Metaphors used sparingly at this time of year. Eliminate similes altogether, save for, 'Green as anything.' May is everything you could ever want from a month.

May 24

But I can guarantee, there'll be no knock on the door
I'm total pro, that's what I'm here for.
When bad things happen to good people. When a beautiful day in May becomes suddenly overcast without warning. Storm up ahead. When Gord gives us the news. Invokes the C-word. Tells us he has Cancer. Brain. Inoperable. When we stop what we're doing and question Everything. When the beloved musician tells us that while there may not be many songs left, he's going to stand and deliver the music he's been preordained to deliver. Come hell or high water. On a beautiful day in May when bad things happen to extraordinary people.
I come from downtown, born ready for you
Armed with will and determination, and grace, too.

May 25

The delivery truck out front. The café door open. The breeze good. Beautiful women are everywhere. Spring dictates the flow of skirt and blouse. Of course they are young and beautiful. I can't help myself. The eye sees what it sees. The reptilian brain knows what it knows. Wants what it wants. The heart flutters. Beats faster. Thankfully, does not stop. Blood in the veins. The breeze shifts. The light, just so. The sky is Viagra blue and maybe I'll get a song out of the remains of the day.

May 26

The things that fall out of our pockets ... little losses never noticed. Precious cargo not really needed. The things that fall out of our pockets. A few shiny coins. A grocery list. The things that fall out of our pockets change our lives. Make us richer. A winter's snow bank is just that: a place to unwittingly deposit a desperate wish for spring. A lover's note changes hands. The things that fall out of our pockets mean everything to the child who spies a flash of silver in the grass. A folded scrap of paper: *Call if you get this note.* A note for a teacher: *Please excuse Jeremy from class this afternoon.*

May 27

Out of our pockets. The things that fall. The possibility of buried treasure. A poem asking forgiveness. A hair pin. An old comb. A tiny note for a friend. A lottery ticket. One secret wish. The things that fall out of our pockets. A grocery list in rhyming couplets:

Bagels bananas a half-litre of cream
Dark chocolate for combustion and a head of steam

Two pieces of salmon and a block of cheese
Some of those and some of these

A wish for a good life for everyone
Some cayenne pepper. A cinnamon bun

If you find this note know I'm ok
Though I was hurting yesterday

But a friend came round and found me here
And an angel whispered in my ear

Please pick up some lettuce and a bag of rice
Some day-old bread at half price

If you find this throw in a pastry if you could
Life's ok — everything's good

May 28

Today, the rain comes down and washes everything away. Everything we thought we knew yesterday. The wind moves the water. Dances the leaves awake on the shoreline. Just the tops of the trees.

May 29

There may not be so many words today. The muse got the wrong address. Return to sender. Hope she found someone else nearby. Not so many words. Just a brown envelope with the promise of a stamp and talk of a journey. A promise in so many words.

May 30

So many words but not today. There may be enough here anyway. Move them around. Shuffle the deck. Mix the metaphor. Find the form that fits. Hold loosely to a whispered promise. A new moon. An old typewriter. Give them more with less. Just ahead a new story. With so many words crowding yesterday's page. The rush to get somewhere fast, gone. Guess there's no hurry now.

May 31

Sun. Clouds. Clouds. Sun. Mood shifts. Moment-to-moment. Wish I may. Wish I might. The morning breaking out in sunlight. Breeze-worthy. Wanting to change myself. Change the world. Notice. Be noticed. Make a difference. Become famous maybe. All before lunch. Clouds. Sun. Sun. Clouds.

June 1

Found a note stuffed in a crack in the wall: *For deep insight please turn over.* It said, *read on.* But the font became an eye chart. The last line a prairie farmhouse burning tiny on the horizon. An ocean of remembered yellow pressing against the windows. Back in town a marching band on sabbatical passes by. Bikers and grad students marching to their own beat. More sunlight. Just the way her hair. Every curve. Always an invitation to unravel in this humidity.

June 2

So many days later and all the ducks lined up just like quack. The planet, as promised, has turned itself in careful but crazy increments toward the Days of Light. The Zenith. Blinded by the. A fall down miracle it always is. The roof of the sky lifts off and blue takes you all the way there and back. Smile. Drink it in. Laugh. Out loud. Recall all those doubts. Relearn how to spell Thank full.

June 3

Grace arrives with little fanfare. A short espresso and a long list of thank yous. Thank You. Thank You. Thank You. I sing you this song. The one I've been working on since the snow banks blocked my view of the bridge and the third verse. Can you hear it now? The lyrics have melted and formed a chorus. And now I know once again why I'm here.

June 4

Learning to love all the time in this new light. All this love in a new time. All this light and love and newness.

June 5

Caution: Even More Word Pairings. Dumb luck. Dead beat. Drip dry. Turn coat. Blood bank. Snow storm. Sea worthy. French kiss. Face off. Fast food. Food fight. Second fiddle. Salt lick. True grit. Lucky charm. Loose change. City slicker. Cat burglar. Car wash. Wide angle. West wing. Young love. Old timer. Burnt offerings. Back waters. Bum steer. Juke box. Jump rope. Kill joy. Cash cow. One way. One world. One love.

June 6

When all goes quiet. Not even the waves. Children waiting for stories that will take them to softer shores and whispery clouds. The river winding and winding. Voices warm and buttery. Drifting. Drifting. Dreaming now. The river winding and winding. Candle glow and whispered prayer. *For rest and food and loving care.*

June 7

See her zoom by on a skateboard in a sundress. Flashing bright through scattered sunlight. Someone spark up a soundtrack to accompany her on her way to possibility. The future lit like a firecracker on a fuse. Everything moving fast and captured by a jittery handheld camera. A blur of tattoo cutting through traffic. Not even a shadow to slow her down. Lean and muscled. Neon tights and a sundress on a skateboard.

June 8

Watch for non-sequiturs. All in favour of juxtapositions. Contradictions, too. When in doubt blend in. Stick your neck out. Be wary of naysayers. It all comes down to this. Savour ambiguity. Honour the middle way. Doff your cap to a trendsetter. You don't have to move that mountain.

June 9

There is a prayer tree growing in your yard. How long you've loved that tree. How long you've never noticed it was there. The wind whispering the branches. The earth and roots practicing faith while no one watches. Wisps of clouds and other invented notation. This is music. This is song. Try to listen for summer and other little promises you've kept all year.

June 10

The way a stand of birch feels sad in a forest of happy. The thin line between Rachmaninoff and rock and roll. The way poetry invites you to say the same thing differently. The belief that just one more cup of coffee. Poets all cramming for the final exam. Words jostling at the starting line. The way friends never fail. Lucky you. You can't wait to tell everyone.

June 11

Heat wave. First memorable one of the season. Heat in waves. Wading pools become tropical getaways. There is a collective equatorial response: people move more slowly. More methodically. Gravitate to watering holes, add ice to whatever they're drinking. Strangely, but not surprisingly, many still hold recent memories of ice that covered lakes and wreaked havoc on roads. Those memories are melting fast. Once upon a time people would have looked for escape from the heat of the city by going for a drive in the country. Maybe they still do. Maybe you're imagining yourself right now: a dog, head poked out of the car window. You picture yourself a handsome dog with a certain amount of dignity despite your tongue hanging out of your mouth, panting. Most likely you're a beagle, ears flapping in the breeze, drooling, the air rushing past making you dizzy with joy.

June 12

Don't we all love friends with cottages? One moment you're urban gridlocked, boxed in by SUV's. The next moment you're on a dock with a gin and tonic concerned only with the requisite amount of precaution necessary to deal with UV's. Better still when the cottage is a cabin. And make no mistake — there is a clear distinction to be made. The contemporary cottage can be a house that happens to be situated near a lake. Big screen television, dishwasher, lawnmower, leaf-blower. These and other conveniences that make going down to the lake or walking in the forest seem inconvenient.

June 13

The cabin blends into its surroundings. The cabin belongs right where it is. Nestled in a stand of white pines that appear to grow directly and impossibly out of large granite outcrops. The Group of Seven has no doubt been to the cabin. Palettes brimming with colour. Enough to paint the Canadian Shield into existence. That the cabin is off-grid is a given. The cabin always needs work. This work may or may not get done. Pleasure lies in the daily labour required to chop wood and carry water.

June 14

At the cabin, there is a red canoe on the shoreline waiting for you. It will show you how to see the night sky and the silky surface of the lake as one. Stars and planets floating above and below. All at once. In the daytime — try early morning or late afternoon — the canoe is willing to show you yourself reflected not only on the surface of the lake but in Every Living Thing that surrounds you.

June 15

Gin and tonics lead to disparaging talk of the beaver. Many unkind words are spoken once the beaver becomes the topic of conversation. As if on cue, there's one motoring across the back bay. Head visible, cutting a line through the water, leaving a quiet wake behind. It belongs to a family of beavers you love to hate. Why? Not because of all the space the beaver took up in your Grade 4 History Lessons: "Describe how the fur trade shaped the development of early Canadian settlement." No, you hate them (and hate does not seem too strong a word) because they are taking down your trees, one beautiful tree at a time. They are industrious creatures. The little bastards will stop at nothing to change the eco-system they share with you while lowering your property values. And thus the need for gin and tonics that lead to disparaging talk of the beaver.

June 16

A flash of kingfisher. Banking over the surface of the lake. Then back up to its favourite perch above the shoreline. A snapping turtle parked on a log in the boggy back bay. A scarlet tanager flitting along the path down to the lake. A pileated woodpecker serves notice from somewhere deeper in the forest. Screen porch rapture. The wind as storyteller. No better time to listen than this moment. Napping always a possibility. Or time to read a book from the cabin archives. Maybe sketch the afternoon light into place. A loose line drawing that feels better than it looks. Eat. Nap. Eat. Nap. Maybe a quick dip when the sun offers an afternoon invitation. The beautiful piercing light of June on the cusp of Solstice. All under the spell of the Canadian Shield.

June 17

Dragon flies helicoptering through the afternoon light. A scatter of blue jays. Blue and noisy. Quiet lapping of water against the dock. An osprey overhead. At the water's edge, the great blue heron impersonating itself. An interactive Zen sculpture. All grace and stillness until it decides to lift off into flight. Nothing to be done about the awkward landing gear that won't retract. Mosquito wine against the screen porch door. Cup of tea or cold beverage? Fiction or non-fiction? Canoe or row boat? These and other demanding decisions.

June 18

Midnight and the barred owl. Otherworldly. Always haunting. And the secret language of tree frogs charting the forest depths. They're either tweeting nonsense or creating a manifesto for addressing global warming. Or both. The call and response of a pair of local whip-poor-wills. Maddening and insistent. A freight train in the distance passing through the high, dark canopy of your dreams.

June 19

The moon rises. The sun is setting. Tonight, in this moment, they share the same evening sky. So close to Solstice anything seems possible. Driving through fields and forests while the planet inches closer to its cosmic apex. Daylight stretches and stretches and stretches. No one dares say it but it feels like this light could go on forever.

June 20

You asked for something other than meaning. Something to make you feel more than the less you so often feel. Images that bear no resemblance to the artwork in your head. Hotel corridor dreams. Pay and display. Park and Fly. Point and shoot. A hot air balloon and a bullet hole. Digging a deeper well. Coming up for air. Reading between the lines. Messing with gravity. Finger on the pulse. Feeling for things just out of reach. Cut off and connected. Feverish headlines. Oceans apart. Lame excuses. Harsh judgements. Tripping over the horizon. Understanding less and less. A shot glass parked right next to the hourglass. Everything running out. A series of complications. Adding new recipes by Braille on this hot skillet of a day.

June 21

To be read quickly without thinking: a familiar degree of sameness. A late arrival. An ethical dilemma of sorts. It's anyone's guess, really. The way the sky looks from here. All the things you used to do. Not in so many words. What would you change anyway? Who will be left to finish what you started? *That wasn't so bad.*

June 22

A length of rebar clamped in a vise of anxiety. Who are you today?

June 23

What are you so scared of? Your own Shadow is a tired old story you drag out again and again and again. Just the thought of meeting darkness on the path is enough to scare the pants off you. A cauldron of shame, guilt, pride, fear, hate, envy, need and greed simmer just below the surface. *That's* what you're so scared of. Your Shadow dragging you and your story out, again and again and again.

June 24

Mark my words. I saw this coming. Yet another referendum to vote on the results of the last referendum. Everybody wants their own country. Everybody wants to make up their own rules. No one looks far enough into the future. No one sees the past coming back around with a sucker punch. They want it all. They want it now. What then? They want more. Things are unraveling. Mark my words.

June 25

Creature comforts. Guilty pleasures. Honesty you've kept to yourself. Overdue books. Things badly handled. Comparing drafts. Editing unwritten stories. Writers blocking your way. Arriving for the first time. Entropy writ large. All the exits sealed. Go to the kitchen cabinet. Random ingredients will do. At the very least write about it.

June 26

Special effects and software engineers. Bells and whistles. Reverb. Tremolo. Digital delay. Difficult decisions made on the last day. Apples and oranges for comparison's sake. Waiting for the final word. Trying and trying to pinpoint the place where problems meet solutions. Be sure to use liner notes sparingly.

June 27

Warm wind and waves. Waves and warm wind. Looking out to Wolfe Island. Sun and sun and sun bouncing off the water. Blue busy perfecting itself out there. I noticed him then. He was parked at the water's edge in a wheelchair watching the wind surfers at work. He seemed to be studying the light. A shore bird considering flight paths old and forgotten. Sails and colourful kites punctuated the day with exclamation marks. The shorebird was aware that wings were not an option. This limitation did nothing to discourage the flight he seemed so intent on capturing. Or perhaps he was considering walking on water.

June 28

The farmer is smiling. The farmer is driving his tractor around his fields in calculated circuits. The farmer's tractor pulls the swather behind it. The swather's blades slice through lush green fields leaving manicured lines of hay in rows, neat and beautiful. The farmer is smiling because the Almanac was bang on this year when it told him the time to cut your hay is NOW. The farmer is not looking over his shoulder scanning the horizon worriedly. There are no lines of black clouds threatening to ruin his yield. There *are* no clouds. Not yesterday. Not today. Not tomorrow. The big round bales will be stacked in the barn dry and seasoning by tomorrow evening. This is money in the bank. This is a holy moment: God smiling on the farmer smiling.

June 29

Dark chocolate can turn a day around. Pass it on. Ask any poet. It's an art of course but the science is deceptively simple. Some disclaimers apply. Be aware, for example, that the amount of dark chocolate required to turn the day around can be a hotly contested debate. A lively discussion that will no doubt fuel rich poetry and provide helpful scientific insights. Pass it on.

June 30

How could you have ever known? What might come from a year's worth of poem? Clichés would suggest one day at a time. Days would suggest line after line. Day-glow paint and shards of glass. Clouds caught in the mountain pass. Follow the words to see where they go. The mundane and miraculous in a jigsaw flow. Asking words to line up in rows. Asking the poet what the poet knows. The manuscript is a mind-map over-grown. With the bits and pieces from a year's worth of poem.

A Caffeinated Postscript

> And pretty soon word spreads that there is a café ... that is wonderful, like a dream, like a mystery, like a painting, and you ought to go there, they will say, for you will never forget it. You will want to stay if you can. Some have for a while.
> — Cynthia Rylant, The Van Gogh Café

I love cafés. I love coffee. I love writing. I love drinking coffee and writing in cafés where I am alone and never alone. Surrounded by people, there is a very special solitude to be found in the busyness and the quiet of a café. I am lucky to live in a place where there are many wonderful spots to drink coffee and write. Sometimes, just talk of espresso is often enough to catapult me into a world of word making. And so I am happily indebted to these coffeehouses where lines and lives unfold — and where many of the pieces in this collection were written.

But there is another very special café I wish to acknowledge and thank for helping bring this book to life. The Bagot Street Café is an underground house of coffee that is a poorly kept secret in my neighbourhood. The doors to the café are (almost) always open. Friends come and go. Cats are fed. Babies are kissed. There is food. There are stories. The espresso is robust as is the company. Love trumps commerce at the Bagot Street Café and I am blessed to be part of the comings and goings. The café feeds me. The café feeds my writing.

Notes

Opening epigraph
Taken from Coleman Barks. (2010). *Rumi. The Big Red Book: The Great Masterpiece Celebrating Mystical Love & Friendship.* HarperCollins. New York.

The stubborn particulars of grace.
Bronwen Wallace. (1987). *The Stubborn Particulars of Grace.* McLellan & Stewart. Toronto, ON.

July 14
Everyday I stare at the world.
Taken from the section, "Work"
Mary Oliver. (2000). *The Leaf and the Cloud. A Poem.* Da Capo Press. Cambridge, MA.

I am thinking: maybe just looking and listening is the real work?
Taken from the section, "From the Book of Time"
Mary Oliver. (2000). *The Leaf and the Cloud. A Poem.* Da Capo Press. Cambridge, MA.

July 18
Pay attention. Be astonished. Tell about it.
From the Poem, "Sometimes"
Mary Oliver. (2009). *Red Bird. Poems.* Beacon Press. Boston, MA.

July 21
Italicized excerpts taken from the Environment Canada Weather website (https://www.weather.gc.ca).

August 3
Random excerpts from the incomparable Frank Zappa
Frank Zappa with Peter Occhiogrosso. (1989). *The Real Frank Zappa Book.* Simon & Schuster. New York.

August 16
What could someone figure out about you by the friends you've chosen? What are the most important things (excluding children) you've brought into the world that would not exist without you?
Gregory Stock. (1987). *The Book of Questions.* Workman Publishing Co. New York.

August 25
Give me my rapture today.
Van Morrison, from the song, "Give me My Rapture Today"
Taken from the 1987 album, *Poetic Champions Compose*

August 30
All the diamonds in this world that mean anything to me/Are conjured up by wind and sunlight sparkling on the sea.
Bruce Cockburn, from the song, "All the Diamonds"
Taken from the 1974 Album *Salt, Sun and Time*

September 26
Walk on down. Walk on down. Walk on down. Walk on down a country road ... Guess my feet know where they want me to go.
James Taylor, from the song, "Country Road"
Taken from the 1970 album, *Sweet Baby James*

October 2
You are ahead by a century. This is our life.
Gord Downie & The Tragically Hip
From the song, "Ahead by a Century"
Taken from the 1996 album, *Trouble at the Henhouse*

November 4
Stephen Harper steps down to make way for Justin Trudeau

November 5
Can we leave enough room for not knowing how it's all going to work out? Pema Chodrin. (2000). *When Things Fall Apart: Heart Advice for Difficult Times.* Shambhala Publications. Boston, MA.

December 17
Peace on earth and mercy mild.
"Hark the Herald Angels Sing"
Lyrics, Charles Wesley, George Whitefield. Music, William H. Cummings

December 22
Above thy deep and dreamless sleep the silent stars go by.
The hopes and fears of all the years are met in Thee tonight.
"O Little Town of Bethlehem"
Lyrics, Philip Brooks. Music, Lewis Redner

December 23
Silent Night. All is calm. All is bright
"Silent Night"
Lyrics, Joseph Mohr. Music, Franz Xaver Gruber

December 24
Not a creature was stirring not even a mouse.
From "The Night Before Christmas" or "Twas the Night Before Christmas" published anonymously in 1823 and later attributed to Clement Clarke Moore.

December 29
Where seldom is heard a discouraging word. And the skies are not cloudy all day.
From the classic American western folk song, "Home on the Range."

December 31
Should auld acquaintance be forgot. And never brought to mind? We'll take a cup of kindness yet for auld lang syne.
From the traditional folk song, "Auld Lang Syne," based on a poem written by Robert Burns.

January 2
One of my favourite Al Purdy poems, "The Freezing Music"
Al Purdy. (1994). *Naked with Summer in Your Mouth*. McClelland & Stewart. Toronto.

January 8
I can feel it coming in the air of night. Oh Lord/And I've been waiting for this moment for all my life. Oh Lord.
Phil Collins, from the song, "In the Air Tonight"
From the 1981 album, *Face Value*

Hello, I must be going!
From Phil Collins's 1982 album, *Hello, I Must be Going.*

January 14
Lacy Mucklow. Illustrated by Angela Porter. (2015). *Portable Color Me Happy: 70 Coloring Templates That Will Make You Smile*. Quarto Publishing Group USA.

January 29
Adrienne Rich. (1991). *An Atlas of the Difficult World. Poems 1988-1991*. W.W. Norton & Company. New York.

February 5
One of my favourite Al Purdy poems, "The Freezing Music"
Al Purdy. (1994). *Naked with Summer in Your Mouth*. Toronto. McClelland & Stewart. Toronto.

The best game you can name
Stompin' Tom Connors. "The Hockey Song"
From the 1973 album, *Stompin' Tom & The Hockey Song*

February 7
Don't be swayed by external circumstances. Don't misinterpret. Don't vacillate. Train wholeheartedly. Don't wallow in self-pity. Don't be jealous. Don't be frivolous. Don't expect applause.
Pema Chodrin. (2000). *When Things Fall Apart: Heart Advice for Difficult Times*. Shambhala Publications. Boston, MA.

February 9
I simply remember my favourite things and then I don't feel so bad.
Taken from the song, "My Favourite Things"
Rodger and Hammerstein (1959) Musical, *The Sound of Music*.

February 12
And the radio plays that forgotten song.
Golden Earring. From the song, "Radar Love"
Taken from the 1973 album, *Moontan*

February 14
Italicized excerpts taken from the Environment Canada Weather website (https://www.weather.gc.ca).

February 23
Italicized excerpts taken from the Environment Canada Weather website (https://www.weather.gc.ca).

February 25
A fun, little story I have read to my children many, many times.
Sam McBratney. (1995). *Guess How Much I Love You*. Candlewick Press. Somerville, MA.

February 27
Step with great care and great tact. And remember that life's a great balancing act.
Dr. Seuss. (1990). *Oh, The Places You'll Go!* Random House. New York.

February 28
If things start happening, don't worry, don't stew. Just go right along and you'll start happening too.
Dr. Seuss. (1990). *Oh, The Places You'll Go!* Random House. New York.

February 29
When a man makes up a story for his child/He becomes a father and a child together, listening.
Coleman Barks. (2010). *Rumi. The Big Red Book: The Great Masterpiece Celebrating Mystical Love & Friendship.* HarperCollins. New York.

March 2
And the wisdom to know the difference
The last line, taken from "The Serenity Prayer"

March 11
It's not just me and it's not just you, this is all around the world.
From the song, "The Myth of Fingerprints"
Taken from Paul Simon's 1986 album, *Graceland*

March 19
Nothing in particular and everything in between
From the song, "You and the Mona Lisa"
Taken from Shawn Colvin's 1996 album, *A Few Small Repairs*

March 22
This is not a day for asking questions, not a day on any calendar …
… The rest of this poem is too blurry for them to read
Coleman Barks. (2010). *Rumi. The Big Red Book: The Great Masterpiece Celebrating Mystical Love & Friendship.* HarperCollins. New York.

March 24
24 and there's so much more
From the song, "Old Man"
Taken from Neil Young's 1971 album, *Harvest*

April 3
Song is not a luxury but a necessary way of being in the world.
Mark Nepo. (2000). *The Book of Awakening.* Conari Press. San Francisco.

April 10
I was desperately unhappy trying to adjust to the world.
Al Purdy. Source unknown.

April 12
One note can go a long way if it's the right one.
Excerpt from guitarist and electronics pioneer, Les Paul
Philip Toshio Sudo. (1997). *Zen Guitar*. Simon & Schuster. New York.

April 13
Metaphors mentioning the moon have no effect on the moon.
Coleman Barks. (2010). *Rumi. The Big Red Book: The Great Masterpiece Celebrating Mystical Love & Friendship*. HarperCollins. New York.

April 28
This entry dedicated to the esteemed and beloved Canadian poet, Lorna Crozier

May 24
But I can guarantee, there'll be no knock on the door
I'm total pro, that's what I'm here for …
… I come from downtown, born ready for you
Armed with will and determination, and grace, too.
From the song, "And Grace, Too"
Taken from the Tragically Hip's 1994 album *Day for Night*

June 6
For rest and food and loving care
Taken from a beloved nighttime prayer, *Father, We Thank Thee* credited to Rebecca Watson (1890).

A Caffeinated Postscript
And pretty soon words spreads that there is a café …
Cynthia Rylant. (1995). *The Van Gogh Café*. Harcourt Brace & Company. New York.

Other Books by Gary Rasberry

As Though it Could be Otherwise
Studio 22 Idea Manufactory, 2011

More Naked than Ever
Hidden Brook Press, 2013

Acknowledgments

I wish to thank my family—Hayden and Zinta and Rena—for their ongoing love and support. I thank Heidi Mack for the artwork that graces the front cover of this book and Diane Black for taking the artwork and creating and designing a beautiful cover. I thank the Bagot Street Café and its patrons for their generous listening to many informal readings of the work that would end up in this collection. I thank both Phil Hall and Bruce Kauffman for their careful reading and editorial work. And, finally, my thanks to Rena Upitis and Wintergreen Studios Press for support in publishing this work.

Wintergreen Studios Press is an independent literary press. It is affiliated with the not-for-profit educational retreat centre, Wintergreen Studios, and supports the work of Wintergreen Studios by publishing works related to education, the arts, and the environment.

www.wintergreenstudios.com

www.ingramcontent.com/pod-product-compliance
Lightning Source LLC
Chambersburg PA
CBHW020935090426
42736CB00010B/1143